No Excuses!

No Excuses!

The Power of Self-Discipline

BRIAN TRACY

Vanguard Press
A Member of the Perseus Books Group

Published by Vanguard Press
A Member of the Perseus Books Group

Designed by Pauline Brown
Set in 11.5 point Sabon

Library of Congress Cataloging-in-Publication Data

Tracy, Brian.
No excuses! : the power of self-discipline for success in your life / Brian Tracy.
p. cm.
ISBN 978-1-59315-582-7 (alk. paper)
1. Self-control. 2. Self-management (Psychology) 3. Success. 4. Success in business. I. Title.
BF632.T72 2010
158.1—dc22

2009054399

PB ISBN: 978-1-59315-632-9

Vanguard Press books are available at special discounts for bulk purchases in the U.S. by corporations, institutions, and other organizations. For more information, please contact the Special Markets Department at the Perseus Books Group, 2300 Chestnut Street, Suite 200, Philadelphia, PA 19103, or call (800) 810-4145, ext. 5000, or e-mail special.markets@perseusbooks.com.

10 9 8 7 6

This book is fondly dedicated
to my friend and partner Eric Berman,
one of the most disciplined and
determined people I have ever met.

Contents

Introduction: The Miracle of Self-Discipline

"There are a thousand excuses for failure but never a good reason."
—Mark Twain

Why are some people more successful than others? Why do some people make more money, live happier lives, and accomplish much more in the same number of years than the great majority? What is the real "secret of success?"

Often I begin a seminar with a little exercise. I ask the audience, "How many people here would like to double their income?"

Almost everyone smiles and raises their hands. I then ask, "How many people here would like to lose weight? Get out of debt? Achieve financial independence?"

Again, everyone smiles, some people cheer, and they all raise their hands. Then I say, "Wonderful! These are great goals that everyone has. We all want to make more money, spend more time with our families, be fit and trim, and achieve financial independence.

"Not only do we all want the same things, but we all know what we have to do to achieve them. And we all intend to do those things, ***sometime***. But before we get started, we decide that we need to take a little vacation to a wonderful fantasy place called 'Someday Isle.'

"We say that 'Someday I'll read that book. Someday I'll start that exercise program. Someday I'll upgrade my skills and earn more money. Someday I'll get my finances under control and get out of debt. Someday I'll do all those things that I know I need to do to achieve all my goals. Someday.'"

Probably 80 percent of the population lives on Someday Isle most of the time. They think and dream and fantasize about all the things they are going to do "someday."

And who are they surrounded by on Someday Isle? Other people on Someday Isle! And what is the chief topic of conversation on Someday Isle? Excuses! They all sit around and swap excuses for being on the island.

"Why are you here?" they ask each other.

Not surprising, their excuses are largely the same: "I didn't have a happy childhood," "I didn't get a good education," "I don't have any money," "My boss is really critical," "My marriage is no good," "No one appreciates me," or "The economy is terrible."

They have come down with the disease of "excusitis," which is invariable fatal to success. They all have good intentions, but as everyone knows, "The road to hell is paved with good intentions."

The first rule of success is simple: Vote yourself off the island!

No more excuses! Do it or don't do it—but don't make excuses. Stop using your incredible brain to think up elaborate rationalizations and justifications for not taking action. Do something. Do anything. Get on with it! Repeat to yourself: "If it's to be, it's up to me!"

Losers make excuses; winners make progress. Now, how can you tell if your favorite excuse is valid or not? It's simple. Look around and ask, "Is there anyone else who has my same excuse who is successful anyway?"

When you ask this question, if you are honest, you will have to admit that there are thousands and even millions of people who have had it far worse than you have who have gone on to do wonderful things with their lives. And what thousands and millions of others have done, you can do as well—if you try.

It has been said that if people put as much energy into achieving their goals as they spend making up excuses for failure, they would actually surprise themselves. But first, you have to vote yourself off the island.

Humble Beginnings

Very few people start off with many advantages. Personally, I did not graduate from high school. I worked at laboring jobs for several years. I had limited education, limited skills, and a limited future. And then I began asking that question: "Why are some people more successful than others?" This question changed my life.

Over the years, I have read thousands of books and articles on the subjects of success and achievement. It seems that the reasons for these accomplishments have been discussed and written about for more than 2,000 years, in every conceivable way.

One quality that most philosophers, teachers, and experts agree on is the importance of self-discipline. Discipline is what you must have to resist the lure of excuses.

It is self-discipline that enables you to "vote yourself off the island." It is the key to a great life and, without it, no lasting success is possible.

The development of self-discipline changed my life, and it will change yours as well. By continually demanding more from myself, I became successful in sales and then in management. I caught up on my schooling and took an MBA degree in my thirties, which required thousands of hours of determined study. I imported Suzuki vehicles into Canada before anyone else, set up sixty-five dealerships, and sold $25 million worth of the vehicles, and this is all after I had started with no knowledge of the industry. What I had, however, was the discipline and determination to learn what I needed to know and then apply what I needed to do.

I got into real estate development with no knowledge or experience, applied the power of discipline, which was then backed by hundreds of hours of work and study. I then went on to build shopping centers, industrial parks, office buildings, and residential subdivisions.

With self-discipline, I have built successful businesses in training, consulting, speaking, writing, recording, and distribution. My audio and video programs, books, seminars, and training programs have sold more than $500 million in thirty-six languages and fifty-four countries. Over the years I have consulted for more than 1,000 companies and trained more than 5 million people in live seminars and talks. In every case, the practice of self-discipline has been essential to my success.

I discovered that you can achieve almost any goal you set for yourself if you have the discipline to pay the price, to do what you need to do, and to never give up.

Who Should Read This Book?

This book is written for ambitious, determined men and women who want to achieve everything that is possible for them in life. It is written for people who are "hungry" to do more, to have more, and to be more than they ever have been before.

Perhaps the most important insight of all with regard to success is that to achieve greatly, you must become a different person. It is not the material things you accomplish or acquire that matter so much as it is the ***quality of the person you must become*** to accomplish well above the average. The development of self-discipline is the high road that makes everything possible for you.

This book will serve as your step-by-step guide to becoming a remarkable person who is capable of remarkable achievements.

• • •

A Chance Encounter Reveals the Reason for Success

Some years ago, I was attending a conference in Washington, D.C. During the lunch break I was eating at a nearby Food Fair. The area was crowded, so I sat down at the last open table by myself, even though it was a table for four.

A few minutes later, an older gentlemen and a younger woman who appeared to be his assistant came along, carrying trays of food and obviously looking for a place to sit.

Having lots of room at my table, I immediately arose and invited the older gentlemen to join me. He was hesitant, but I insisted. Finally, he sat down, quite thankfully, and we began to chat over lunch.

It turned out that his name was Kop Kopmeyer. As it happened, I immediately knew who he was. He was a legend in the field of success and achievement. Kop Kopmeyer had written four bestselling books, each of which contained 250 success principles that he had derived from more than fifty years of research and study. I had read all four books from cover to cover, each more than once.

After we had chatted for a while, I asked him the question that many people in this situation would ask: "Of all the 1,000 success principles that you have discovered, which do you think is the most important?"

He smiled at me with a twinkle in his eye, as if he had been asked this question many times, and he replied without hesitating, "The most important success principle of all was stated by Elbert Hubbard, one of the most prolific writers in American history, at the beginning of the twentieth century. He said, '***Self-discipline is the ability to do what you should do, when you should do it, whether you feel like it or not.***'"

He went on to say, "There are 999 other success principles that I have found in my reading and experience, but without self-discipline, none of them work. With self-discipline, they all work."

Thus, self-discipline is the key to personal greatness. It is the magic quality that opens all doors for you and makes everything else possible. With self-discipline, the average person can rise as far and as fast as his talents and intelligence can take him. But without self-discipline, a person with every blessing of background, education, and opportunity will seldom rise above mediocrity.

Your Two Worst Enemies

Just as self-discipline is the key to success, the *lack* of self-discipline is the major cause of failure, frustration, underachievement, and unhappiness in life. It causes us to make excuses and sell ourselves short.

Perhaps the two biggest enemies of success, happiness and personal fulfillment, are first the Path of Least Resistance and, second, the Expediency Factor.

The Path of Least Resistance is what causes people to take the easy way in almost every situation. They seek shortcuts to everything. They arrive at work at the last minute and leave at the first opportunity. They look for get-rich-quick schemes and easy money. Over time, they develop the habit of always seeking an easier, faster way to get the things they want rather than doing what is hard but necessary to achieve real success.

The Expediency Factor, which is an extension of the law of least resistance, is even worse when leading people to failure and underachievement. This principle says, "People invariably seek the fastest and easiest way to get the things they want, right now, with little or no concern for the long-term consequences of their behaviors." In other words, most people do what is ***expedient,*** what is fun and easy rather than what is ***necessary*** for success.

Every day, and every minute of every day, there is a battle going on inside of you between doing what is right, hard, and necessary (like the angel on one shoulder) or doing what is fun, easy, and of little or no value (like the devil on your other shoulder). Every minute of every day, you must fight and win this battle with the Expediency Factor and resist the pull of the Path of Least Resistance if you truly desire to become everything you are capable of becoming.

Take Control of Yourself

Another definition of self-discipline is ***self-mastery***. Success is possible only when you can master your own emotions, appetites, and inclinations. People who lack the ability to master their appetites become weak and dissolute, as well as unreliable in other things as well.

Self-discipline can also be defined as ***self-control.*** Your ability to control yourself and your actions, control what you say and do, and ensure that your behaviors are consistent with your long-term goals and objectives is the mark of the superior person.

Discipline has been defined as ***self-denial.*** This requires that you deny yourself the easy pleasures, the temptations that lead so many people astray, and instead discipline yourself to do only those things that you know are right for the long term and appropriate for the moment.

Self-discipline requires ***delayed gratification***, the ability to put off satisfaction in the short term in order to enjoy greater rewards in the long term.

Think Long Term

Sociologist Dr. Edward Banfield of Harvard University conducted a fifty-year study into the reasons for upward socioeconomic mobility in America. He concluded that the most important single attribute of people who achieved great success in life was "long time perspective." Banfield defined "time perspective" as "the amount of time an individual takes into consideration when determining his present actions."

In other words, the most successful people are long-term thinkers. They look into the future as far as they can to determine the kind of people they want to become and the goals they want to achieve. They then come back to the present and determine the things that they will have to do—or not do—to achieve their desired futures.

This practice of long-term thinking applies to work, career, marriage, relationships, money, and personal conduct—each of which is covered in the pages ahead. Successful people make sure that everything they do in the short term is consistent with where they want to end up in the long term. They practice self-discipline at all times.

Perhaps the most important word in long-term thinking is ***sacrifice***. Superior people have the ability to throughout their lives make sacrifices in the short term, both large and small, so as to assure greater results and rewards in the long term.

You see this willingness to sacrifice in people who spend many hours and even years preparing, studying, and upgrading their skills to make themselves more valuable so that they can have a better life in the future, rather than spending most of their time socializing and having fun in the present.

Longfellow once wrote:

"Those heights by great men, won and kept,
Were not achieved by sudden flight.
But they, while their companions slept,
Were toiling upward in the night."

Your ability to think, plan, and work hard in the short term and to discipline yourself to do what is right and necessary before you do what is fun and easy is the key to creating a wonderful future for yourself.

Your ability to think long term is a developed skill. As you get better at it, you become more able to predict with increasing accuracy what is likely to happen to you in the future as the result of your actions in the present. This is a quality of the superior thinker.

Short-Term Gain Can Cause Long-Term Pain

There are two laws that you fall victim to when you fail to practice self-discipline. The first is called the "Law of Unintended Consequences." This law states that "the unintended consequences of an action can be far worse than the intended consequences of that behavior because of a lack of long-term thinking."

The second is the "Law of Perverse Consequences," which says that "a short-term action aimed at immediate gratification can lead to perverse, or the opposite, consequences from those at which it was aimed."

For example, you might make an investment of time, money, or emotion with the desire and intent to be better off and happier as a result. But because you acted without carefully thinking or doing your homework, the consequences of your behavior turned out to be far worse than if you had done nothing at all. Every person has had this experience, and usually more than once.

The Common Denominator of Success

Herbert Grey, a businessman, conducted a long-term study searching for what he called "the common denominator of success." After eleven years, he finally concluded that the common denominator of success was that "successful people make a ***habit*** of doing the things that unsuccessful people don't like to do."

And what were these things? It turned out that the things that successful people don't like to do are the same things that failures don't like to do either. But successful people do them anyway because they know that this is the price they have to pay if they want to enjoy greater success and rewards in the future.

What Grey found was that successful people are more concerned with "pleasing results," whereas failures were more concerned about "pleasing methods." Successful, happy people were more concerned with the ***positive, long-term consequences of their behaviors,*** whereas unsuccessful people were more concerned with ***personal enjoyment and immediate gratification.***

Motivational speaker Denis Waitley has said that the top people were those who were more concerned with activities that were "goal achieving," whereas average people were more concerned with activities that were "tension relieving."

Dinner Before Dessert

The simplest rule in the practice of self-discipline is to eat "dinner before dessert." In a meal, there is a logical order of dishes, and dessert comes last. First, you eat the main courses and clean your plate; only then do you have dessert.

There is a cute but misleading bumper sticker that says, "Life is short; eat dessert first."

Just think what would happen if you came home after work and, instead of eating a healthy dinner, you ate a large piece of apple pie with ice cream. What kind of appetite for healthy, nutritious food would you have afterward? With all that sugar in your stomach, how would you feel? Would you feel re-energized and eager to do something productive? Or would you feel tired and sluggish and ready to write off the day as largely finished?

You get the same result when you go for a drink or two after work and then come home and turn on the television. These are simply different forms of "dessert" that largely eliminate your ability to do anything useful for the rest of the evening.

Perhaps the worst part of all is that, whatever you do repeatedly soon becomes a ***habit.*** And a habit, once formed, is hard to break. The habit of taking the easy way, doing what is fun and enjoyable, or eating dessert before dinner becomes stronger and stronger, and it leads inevitably to personal weakness, underachievement, and failure.

The Habit of Self-Discipline

Fortunately, you can develop the habit of self-discipline. The regular practice of disciplining yourself to do what you should do, when you should do it, whether you feel like it or not becomes stronger and stronger as you practice it. You refuse to make excuses.

Bad habits are easy to form, but hard to live with. Good habits are hard to form, but easy to live with. And as Goethe said, "Everything is hard before it's easy."

It is hard to form the habits of self-discipline, self-mastery, and self-control, but once you have developed them, they become automatic and easy to practice. When the habits of self-discipline are firmly entrenched in your behavior, you start to feel uncomfortable when you are not behaving in a self-disciplined manner.

The best news is that all habits are ***learnable.*** You can learn any habit you need to learn in order to become the kind of person that you want to become. You can become an excellent person by practicing self-discipline whenever it is called for.

Every practice of self-discipline ***strengthens*** every other discipline. Unfortunately, every weakness in discipline weakens your other disciplines as well.

To develop the habit of self-discipline, you first make a firm decision about how you will behave in a particular area of activity. You then refuse to allow exceptions until the habit of self-discipline in that area is firmly established. Each time you slip, as you will, you resolve once again to keep practicing self-discipline until it becomes easier for you to behave in a disciplined way than to behave in an undisciplined way.

The Big Payoff

The payoff for developing high levels of self-discipline is extraordinary! There is a direct relationship between self-discipline and ***self-esteem***:

- The more you practice self-mastery and self-control, the more you like and value yourself;
- The more you discipline yourself, the greater is your sense of self-respect and personal pride;
- The more you practice self-discipline, the better is your self-image. You see yourself and think about yourself in a more positive way. You feel happier and more powerful as a person.

The development and maintenance of the habit of self-discipline are a lifelong task, an ongoing battle. It never ends. The temptation to follow the path of least resistance and the expediency factor lurk continually in the back of your mind. They are always waiting for an opportunity to pounce, to lead you astray into doing what is fun, easy, and unimportant rather than what is hard, necessary, and life-enhancing.

Napoleon Hill concluded his bestselling book of the same name by saying that "Self-discipline is ***the master key to riches***." Self-discipline is the key to self-esteem, self-respect, and personal pride. The development of self-discipline is your guarantee that you will eventually overcome all your obstacles and create a wonderful life for yourself.

The ability to practice self-discipline is the real reason why some people are more successful and happy than others.

How This Book Is Written

In the pages ahead, I will describe the twenty-one areas of life in which the practice of self-discipline is vital to fulfilling your full potential and achieving everything that is possible for you.

This book is divided into three sections for greater ease of use. Part I is entitled "Self-Discipline and Personal Success." In these seven chapters, you will learn how to release more and more of your ***personal potential*** by practicing self-discipline in every area of your personal life, including setting goals, building character, accepting responsibility, developing courage, and backing everything you do with persistence and determination.

In the seven chapters of Part 2, you will learn how to achieve vastly more than ever before in the areas of ***business, sales, and personal finance***. You learn why and how self-discipline is essential to becoming a leader in your field, to operating a business more profitably, to making more sales, investing more intelligently, and managing your time for maximum results.

Finally, in the seven chapters of Part 3, you will learn how to apply the miracle of self-discipline to your ***personal life***. You will learn how to practice self-discipline in the areas of happiness, health, fitness, marriage, children, friendship, and the attainment of peace of mind. You will learn how to enhance the quality of your life and your relationships in every area.

In each chapter, I will to show you how you can incorporate higher levels of self-discipline and self-mastery into everything you do.

In the pages ahead, you will learn how to take complete control over your own personal and professional development and how to become a stronger, happier, more self-confident person in every area of your life that is important to you. You will learn how to break old habits that may be holding you back and how to develop the habits of self-reliance, self-determination, and self-discipline that will enable you to set and achieve any goal. You will learn how to take complete control over your mind, your emotions, and your future.

When you master the power of self-discipline, you will become ***unstoppable***, like a force of nature. You will never make excuses for not making progress. You will accomplish more in the next few months and years than most people accomplish in a lifetime.

PART I

Self-Discipline and Personal Success

Your success in life depends more on the person you become than on the things you do or acquire. As Aristotle wrote, "The ultimate end of life is the development of character." In these chapters, you will learn how to develop and use discipline in order to become an excellent person. You will learn how to develop greater self-esteem, self-respect, and personal pride. You will learn the essential disciplines required for personal greatness and how to build them into your own character and personality.

Chapter 1

Self-Discipline and Success

"The first and best victory is to conquer self."
—PLATO

Why do some people accomplish so much more in their personal and professional lives than others? This question has occupied some of the very best minds throughout human history. More than 2,300 years ago, Aristotle wrote that the ultimate aim of human life is to be happy. He said that the great question that each of us must answer is, ***"How shall we live in order to be happy?"***

Your ability to ask and answer that question correctly for yourself—and then to follow where your answer leads you—will largely determine whether you achieve your own happiness, and how soon.

Begin with your own personal definition. How do ***you*** define success? If you could wave a magic wand and make your life perfect in every way, what would it look like?

Describe Your Ideal Life

If your ***business, work, and career*** were ideal in every way, what would they look like? What would you be doing? What sort of company would you work for? What position would you have? How much money would you earn? What kind of people would you work with? And, especially, what would you need to do more or less of to create your perfect career?

If your ***family life*** were perfect in every way, what would it look like? Where would you live, and how would you be living? What kind of a lifestyle would you have? What sort of things would you want to have and do with the members of your family? If you had no limitations and you could wave a magic wand, in what ways would you change your family life today?

If your ***health*** were perfect, how would you describe it? How would you feel? How much would you weigh? How would your levels of health and fitness be different from what they are today? Most of all, what steps could you take immediately to begin moving toward your ideal levels of health and energy?

If your ***financial situation*** were ideal, how much would you have in the bank? How much would you be earning each month and each year from your investments? If you had enough money that you never had to worry about finances again, how much would that be? What steps could you take, starting today, to create your ideal financial life?

• • •

Do Your Own Thing

A popular definition of success is "being able to live your life in your own way, doing only those things that you want to do, with the people who you choose, in the situations you desire."

In each case, when you begin to define what "success" means to you, you can immediately see things that you should be doing more of or less of in order to begin creating your ideal life. And the biggest thing that holds you back from moving in the direction of your dreams is usually your favorite excuses and a lack of self-discipline.

It's not that you don't know ***what*** to do, but rather that you don't have the ***discipline*** to make yourself do what you should do, whether you feel like it or not.

Join the Top 20 Percent

In our society, the top 20 percent of people earn 80 percent of the money and enjoy 80 percent of the riches and rewards. This "Pareto Principle" has been proven over and over again since it was first formulated in 1895 by Vilfredo Pareto. Your first goal in your career should be to get into the top 20 percent in your chosen field.

In the twenty-first century, there is a premium on knowledge and skill. The more knowledge you acquire and the greater skill that you apply, the more competent and valuable you become. As you get better at what you do, your income-earning ability increases—like compound interest.

Unfortunately, the majority of people—the bottom 80 percent—make little or no effort to upgrade their skills. Most people, according to Geoffrey Colvin's 2009 book *Talent Is Overrated,* learn their jobs in the first year of their employment, and then they never get any better. It is only the top people in every field who are committed to continuous improvement.

Because of this increasing disparity of productive ability, based on knowledge, skill, and hard work, the top 1 percent of people in American today control as much as 33 percent of the financial assets.

Starting with Nothing

Interestingly, almost everyone starts out the same in life—with little or nothing. Almost all fortunes in America (and worldwide) are ***first*** generation. This means that most individuals started with little or nothing and earned everything they own in their current lifetime.

The wealthiest people in America are almost all first-generation multibillionaires. This is the case with wealthy Americans such as Bill Gates, Warren Buffett, Larry Ellison, Michael Dell, and Paul Allen. Fully 80 percent of millionaires and multimillionaires started with little money, often penniless, and sometimes deeply in debt and with few advantages, such as Sam Walton, who died worth more than $100 billion. Why have these people been able to achieve so much when so many have achieved so little?

In their book, ***The Millionaire Next Door,*** Thomas Stanley and William Danko interviewed more than 500 millionaires and surveyed 11,000 more over a twenty-five-year period. They asked them why they felt they had been able to achieve financial independence when most of the people around them, who started at the same place, were still struggling. Fully 85 percent of this new generation of millionaires replied by saying something like "I didn't have a better education or more intelligence, but I was willing to work ***harder*** than anyone else."

Hard Work Is the Key

The indispensable requirement for hard work is self-discipline. Success is possible only when you can overcome the natural tendency to cut corners and take the easy way. Lasting success is possible only when you can discipline yourself to work hard for a long, long time.

As I mentioned in the Introduction, I started my own life with no money or advantages. For years, I worked at laboring jobs, at which I earned just enough to get from paycheck to paycheck. I stumbled into sales when I could no longer find a laboring job, where I spun my wheels for many months before I began asking that question: "Why is it that some people are more successful in selling than others?"

One day, a top salesman then told me that the top 20 percent of salespeople earn 80 percent of the money. I had never heard that before. This meant that the bottom 80 percent of salespeople had to be satisfied with the remaining 20 percent, with what was left over after the top people had taken the lion's share. I decided then and there that I was going to be in the top 20 percent. This decision changed my life.

The Great Law

Then I learned the "Iron Law of the Universe," which made getting into the top 20 percent possible. It was the Law of Cause and Effect, or sowing and reaping. This law says that "for every effect, there is a specific cause or series of causes."

This law says that if you want to achieve success in any area, you must determine how success is achieved in that area and then practice those skills and activities repeatedly until you achieve the same results.

Here's the rule: "If you ***do*** what other successful people do, over and over again, nothing can stop you from eventually enjoying the same rewards that they do. But if you ***don't*** do what successful people do, nothing can help you."

The law of sowing and reaping, from the Old Testament, is a variation of The Law of Cause and Effect. It says that "whatsoever a man soweth, that also shall he reap." This law says that whatever you put in, you get out. It also says that whatever you are reaping today is a result of what you have sown in the past. So if you are not happy with your current "crop," it is up to you, starting today, to plant a ***new*** crop, to begin doing more of those things that lead to success—and to stop engaging in those activities that lead nowhere.

• • •

Success Is Predictable

Success is not an accident. Sadly, failure is not an accident either. You succeed when you do what other successful people do, over and over, until these behaviors become a habit. Likewise, you fail if you don't do what successful people do. In either case, nature is ***neutral***. Nature does not take sides. Nature doesn't care. What happens to you is simply a matter of law—the law of cause and effect.

You can look at yourself as a machine with a ***default*** mechanism. Your default mechanism is the almost irresistible attraction of the expediency factor and the path of least resistance that I described in the Introduction. In the absence of self-discipline, your default mechanism goes off automatically. This is the main cause of underachievement and the failure to realize your true potential.

When you are not working ***deliberately, consciously,*** and ***continuously*** to do, be, and have those things that constitute success for you, your default mechanism is at work. You end up doing those fun, easy, and low-value things in the short term that lead to frustration, financial worries, and failure in the long term.

The Secrets of Success

The great oil man, H. L. Hunt, who was at one time the richest self-made billionaire in the world, was once asked by a television journalist for his "secrets of success." He replied: "There are only three requirements for success. First, decide exactly what it is you want in life. Second, determine the price that you are going to have to pay to get the things you want. And third, and this is most important, resolve to pay that price."

One of the most important requirements for success, once you have decided what it is that you want, is the quality of ***willingness.*** Successful people are willing to pay the price, whatever it is and for as long as it takes, until they achieve the results they desire.

Everyone wants to be successful. Everyone wants to be healthy, happy, thin, and rich. But most people are not willing to pay the price. Occasionally, they may be willing to pay ***part*** of the price, but they are not willing to pay the ***whole*** price. They always hold back. They always have some excuse or rationalization for not disciplining themselves to do everything that they need to do to achieve their goals.

Pay the Price

How can you tell when you have paid the full price of success? It's simple: Look around you. There it is! You can always tell how much of the price of success you have paid by looking at your current lifestyle and your bank account. By the Law of Correspondence, your outer world will, like a mirror, always reflect the person you are and the price you have paid on the ***inside.***

There is an interesting point about the price of success: It must always be paid in full—and ***in advance.*** Success, however you define it, is not like a restaurant where you pay ***after*** you have enjoyed your meal. Instead it is like a cafeteria, where you can choose whatever you want, but you must pay for it before you eat it.

Motivational speaker Zig Ziglar says, "The elevator to success is out of order, but the stairs are always open."

Learn from the Experts

Kop Kopmeyer, who I mentioned in the Introduction, also told me that the second most important success principle, after self-discipline, is that you must "learn from the experts. You will never live long enough to learn it all for yourself."

If you want to be successful, your first job is to learn what you need to learn in order to achieve the success you desire. Learn from the experts. Read their books. Listen to their audio programs. Attend their seminars. Write to them or approach them directly and ask them for advice. Sometimes, one idea is all you need to change the direction of your life. Let me give you an example of what I mean:

> Some years ago, I was referred by a friend to an excellent dentist. I learned later that he had a superb reputation. He was called the "dentist's dentist." He was the dentist that the other dentists went to when they needed excellent dental work. He told me that he attended every major dental conference that he could. When he was there, he attended every session, listening to dentists from all the over the country, and all over the world, discuss the latest breakthroughs in dental technology.
>
> One week, at great sacrifice in time and money, he attended an international dental conference in Hong Kong. At that conference, he sat in on a session given by a Japanese dentist who had discovered a new technology in

> cosmetic surgery that improved the appearance of teeth and enabled people to look handsome or beautiful indefinitely.
>
> He returned to San Diego and immediately began using the new technique in his practice. Soon, he became excellent in this area and developed a national reputation. Within a couple of years, people were coming to him from all over southwestern United States for this treatment. Because he had developed this expertise, he could raise his fees again and again. Eventually, he had made so much money that he was able to retire at the age of fifty-five, financially independent and able to spend the rest of his life with his family, traveling and fulfilling his dreams.

The point of this story is that, by continually seeking out ideas and advice from other experts in his field, he came across a new technology that helped him become the leader in his field and saved him ten years of hard work in order to reach the same level of financial success. This could happen to you as well, but only if you become a lifelong student of your craft.

Mental and Physical Fitness Need to Be *Ongoing*

Achieving success is like achieving physical fitness. It is like bathing, brushing your teeth, and eating. It is something that you need to do continuously, every day. Once you begin, you never stop until your life and career are over and you have achieved all the success you desire.

> Not long ago, I was giving a seminar in Seattle. Just before the break, I encouraged people to buy and listen to

my audio programs on sales, time management, and personal success. At the break, several people came up to me to ask me questions about the seminar content. One salesman pushed his way forward and said, "When you encourage people to buy your programs, you should tell them the whole truth."

I asked, "How do you mean?"

He went on to say, "You are not telling the whole truth about your programs. You should tell people that they only work for a certain period of time, and then they stop working."

Again, I asked, "How do you mean?"

He said, "Well, I came to your seminar about five years ago, and I was completely convinced by your presentation. I bought all your programs and began listening to them. I read every day in sales. And you were right, over the next three years, I tripled my income and became the top seller in my company. But then my income flattened out and has not increased at all over the last two years. The fact is that your materials stop working after a certain point."

I then asked him, "What happened to you two years ago, when your income flattened out and stopped increasing?"

He searched his memory, thought for a while and then said, "Well, I was selling so much that I was hired away by another company. Ever since I started my new job, my income has remained flat."

I asked him, "What did you do differently in your new job in comparison with your previous job?"

He started to answer. He then stopped. A shocked look came over his face. Finally he replied, "Oh my gosh! I stopped doing it. When I changed jobs, I stopped reading in sales. I stopped listening to audio programs. I stopped attending seminars. I stopped doing it!"

He walked away shaking his head, muttering to himself, "I stopped doing it. I stopped doing it. I stopped doing it."

Becoming an expert in your field, continually upgrading your skills—which I will talk about in Chapter 5—is like physical fitness. If you stop exercising for any period of time, you don't maintain your fitness at the same level. You begin to decline. Your body and your muscles become softer and weaker. You lose your strength, flexibility, and stamina. In order to maintain them, you must keep working at them every day, every week, and every month.

Become All You Can Be

There is an even more important reason for you to practice the self-discipline that leads onward and upward to the great successes that are possible for you. The practice of self-discipline enables you to change your ***character***, to become a stronger and better person. The exercise of self-discipline has a powerful effect on your mind and emotions, developing you into a different person from the one that you would have been without self-discipline.

Imagine yourself in a chemistry lab. You mix a series of chemicals in a Petri dish and put it over a Bunsen burner. The Bunsen burner heats the chemicals to the point at which they crystallize and become hardened. But once you have crystallized these chemicals using intense heat, they cannot be transformed back into liquid form.

In the same way, your personality begins like a liquid: soft, fluid, and formless. But as you apply the heat of self-discipline, as you exert yourself to do what is hard and necessary rather than what is fun and easy, your personality crystallizes and hardens at a higher level as well.

The greatest benefit you enjoy from exerting self-discipline in the pursuit of your goals is that you become a different person. You become stronger and more resolute. You develop greater self-control and determination. You actually shape and strengthen your personality and transform yourself into a better person.

The rule is that "to become someone that you have never been before, you must do something that you have never done before." This means that to develop a superior character, you must exert ever-higher levels of self-discipline and self-mastery on yourself. You must do the things that average people don't like to do.

Another success principle is that "to achieve something that you have never achieved before, you must learn and practice qualities and skills that you have never had before."

By practicing self-discipline, you become a new person. You become better, stronger, and more clearly defined. You develop higher levels of self-esteem, self-respect, and personal pride. You move yourself up the ladder of human evolution and become a person of higher character and resolve.

Success Is Its Own Reward

The wonderful thing about the achievement of success is that every step in that direction is rewarding in itself. Each step you take toward becoming a better person and accomplishing more than you ever have before makes you feel happier, more confident, and more fulfilled.

ou've heard it said that "nothing succeeds like suc- cc.s." What this means is that the greatest reward of success is ***not the money you make*** but rather ***the excellent person you become*** in the process of striving toward success and exerting self-discipline every time it is required.

In the next chapter, I will explain how you can become the truly excellent person you are capable of becoming.

Action Exercises:

Take out a pen right now and write down your answers to the questions below.

1. If your work life and career were ideal, what would they look like? What one discipline could you develop that would help you to achieve it?
2. If your family life were ideal, what would it look like, and what one discipline would help you the most to make it a reality?
3. If your health were perfect in every way, what disciplines would you have that make it possible?
4. If your financial situation were ideal today, what one discipline would you have that would help you the most?
5. Why aren't you *already* as successful as you would like to be, and what one discipline would help you the most to achieve all your goals?
6. What one skill could you develop that would help you to realize more of your goals?
7. If you could wave a magic wand and be completely disciplined in one area, which one discipline would have the greatest positive impact on your life?

Chapter 2

Self-Discipline and Character

"Hold yourself responsible for a higher standard than anyone else expects of you. Never excuse yourself. Never pity yourself. Be a hard master to yourself and be lenient to everyone else."

—HENRY WARD BEECHER,
NINETEENTH-CENTURY CLERGYMAN

The development of character is the great business of life. Your ability to develop a reputation as a person of character and honor is the highest achievement of both social and business life. Ralph Waldo Emerson wrote, "What you do speaks so loudly that I cannot hear a word that you say."

The person you are today, your innermost character, is the sum total of all your choices and decisions in life up to this date. Each time you have chosen rightly and acted consistently with the very best that you know, you have strengthened your character and become a better person. The reverse is also true: Each time you have compromised, taken the easy way, or behaved in a manner inconsistent with what you knew to be right, you have weakened your character and softened your personality.

The Great Virtues

There are a series of virtues or values that are usually possessed by a person of character. These are courage, compassion, generosity, temperance, persistence, and friendliness, among others. We will talk about some of them in Part 3 of this book. Coming before all these values, however, is the most important one of all when determining the depth and strength of your character: ***integrity.***

It is your level of integrity, living in complete truth with yourself and others, that demonstrates more than anything else the quality of your character. In a way, integrity is actually the value that ***guarantees*** all the other values. When your level of integrity is higher, you are more honest with yourself and more likely to live consistently with all the other values that you admire and respect.

However, it takes tremendous self-discipline to become a person of character. It takes considerable willpower to always "do the right thing" in every situation. And it takes both self-discipline and willpower to resist the temptation to cut corners, take the easy way, or act for short-term advantage.

All of life is a ***test***, to see what you are really made of deep, down inside. ***Wisdom*** can be developed in private through study and reflection, but ***character*** can be developed only in the give and take of daily life, when you are forced to choose and decide among alternatives and temptations.

• • •

The Test of Character

It is only when you are under pressure—when you are forced to choose one way or another, to either live consistently with a value or to compromise it—that you demonstrate your true character. Emerson also said, "Guard your integrity as a sacred thing; nothing at last is sacred except the integrity of your own mind."

You are a "choosing organism." You are constantly making choices, one way or the other. Every choice you make is a statement about your true values and priorities. At each moment, you choose what is more important or of higher value to you over what is less important or of lesser value.

The only bulwark against temptation, the path of least resistance, and the expediency factor is character. The only way that you can develop your full character is by exerting your willpower in every situation when you are tempted to do what is easy and expedient rather than what is correct and necessary.

The Big Payoff

The payoff for becoming a person of character, for exerting your willpower and self-discipline to live consistently with the very best that you know, is tremendous. When you choose the higher value over the lower, the more difficult over the easy, the right over the wrong, you feel good about yourself. Your self-esteem increases. You like and respect yourself more. You have a greater sense of personal pride.

In addition to feeling excellent about yourself when you behave with character, you also earn the respect and esteem of all the people around you. They will look up to you and admire you. Doors will be opened for you. People will help you. You will be paid more, promoted faster, and given even greater responsibilities. As you become a person of honor and character, opportunities will appear all around you.

On the other hand, you can have all the intelligence, talent, and ability in the world, but if people do not trust you, you will never get ahead. People will not hire you, and if they do, they will dehire you as soon as possible. Financial institutions will not lend you money. Because "birds of a feather flock together," the only associates (never friends) you will have will be other people of questionable character. Furthermore, since the people you associate with have a major effect on your attitude and personality, you make or break your entire life with the quality of your character—or the lack thereof.

The Development of Character

Aristotle wrote, "All advancement in society begins with the development of the character of the young." This means that advancement in your life begins with the learning and practice of values.

You learn values in one or all of three ways: instruction, study, and practice. Let's look at each of these more closely.

Teach Your Children Values. One of the chief roles of parenting is to teach children values. This requires patient instruction and explaining values to them over and over again as they are growing up. Once is never enough. The value—and the importance of living by that value—must be explained. Parents must not only give illustrations but also contrast the adherence to a value, especially that of telling the truth with its opposite, that of lying or telling half-truths.

Children are very susceptible to the lessons they receive from the important people in their lives as they are growing up. They accept what you say as their parent as a fact, as absolute truth. They absorb what you say like a sponge. You write your description of values on their souls, which are like wet clay, so that what you write becomes a permanent part of the way they see the world and relate to life.

More than anything else, as we'll see in Chapter 19, you demonstrate your values in your ***behavior.*** Your children watch you and strive to emulate the values that you not only teach and preach, but also practice. And they are always watching.

The Rockefeller family children were famous for being taught financial values at an early age. Even though their father was one of the richest men in America, the children were given tasks and chores to perform before they received their allowances. They were then instructed on how to spend their allowances: how to save, how much to give to charity, and how much to invest. As a result, they grew up to become successful businessmen and statesmen, unlike children who had grown up in wealthy homes who were seldom disciplined in money matters.

Study the Values You Admire. You learn values by studying them closely. The Law of Concentration says that "whatever you dwell upon grows and increases in your life."

What this means is that when you study and read stories about men and women who demonstrated the kind of values that you admire and respect, and then think about those stories and that behavior, those values sink ever deeper into your mind. Once these values are "programmed" into your subconscious, they create a propensity within you to behave consistently with those values when the situation requires them.

For example, in military training, soldiers are continually told stories of courage, obedience, discipline, and the importance of supporting their fellow soldiers. The more they hear these stories, discuss them, and think about them, the more likely they are to behave consistently with these values when they are under the pressure of actual combat.

The core virtue of character is ***truth.*** Whenever you tell the truth, however inconvenient it may be at the time, you feel better about yourself and you earn the respect of the people around you. One of the highest accolades you can pay another person is to say that "he or she always tells the truth."

Emulate the People You Most Admire. Much of your character is determined by the people you most admire, both living and dead. Who are they? Looking over your life and history, make a list of the people whom you most admire, and next to their names, write out the virtues or values that they most represent to you.

If you could spend an afternoon with anyone, living or dead, what one person would you choose? Why would you choose that person? What would you talk about during your afternoon together? What questions would you ask, or what would you want to learn?

Consider this as well: Why would that person want to spend an afternoon with ***you***? What are the virtues and values that you have developed that make you a valuable and interesting person? What makes you special?

Practice the Values You Respect. You develop values by practicing them whenever they are called for. As the Roman Stoic philosopher Epictetus said, "Circumstances do not make the man; they merely reveal him to himself."

When a problem occurs, people tend to react automatically based on the highest values that they have developed up to that moment.

We develop values by ***repetition***, by behaving consistently with a particular value over and over again, until it becomes a habit, and locks in so that we come to practice it automatically. Men and women with highly developed characters behave in a manner consistent with their highest values, and they do so without thought or hesitation.

There is no question in their minds about whether or not they are doing the right thing.

The Structure of Personality

The ***psychology*** of character involves the three parts of your personality: your self-ideal, your self-image, and your self-esteem.

Your Self-Ideal. Your self-ideal is that part of your mind composed of your values, virtues, ideals, goals, aspirations, and your idea of the very best person that you can possibly be. In other words, your self-ideal is composed of those values that you most admire in others and most aspire to possess in yourself.

The most important part of your self-ideal is summarized in the word "clarity." Superior people are those who are absolutely clear about who they are and what they believe. They have complete clarity about the values they believe in and what they stand for. They are not confused or indecisive. They are firm and resolute when it comes to any decision in which a value is involved.

On the other hand, weak and irresolute people are fuzzy and unclear about their values. They have only a vague notion of what is right or wrong in any situation. As a result, they take the path of least resistance and act expediently. They do whatever seems to be the fastest and easiest thing to get what they want in the short term, giving little to no consideration or concern about the consequences of their acts.

The Evolution of Character. In biology, life forms are categorized from the least to the most complex, from single-celled plankton all the way up the increasingly complex spectrum of life to the human being. Similarly, human beings can be organized along a spectrum as well, from the least to the most developed. The lowest forms of humans are those with no values, virtues, or character. These people always act expediently and take the path of least resistance in their search for immediate gratification.

At the highest levels of development of the human race, however, are those men and women of complete integrity, who would never compromise their honesty or their character for anything, including the threat of financial loss, pain, or even death.

George Washington is famous for his honesty, which was demonstrated in the story in which he admitted that he had cut down the cherry tree. In the same vein, the founding fathers of the United States wrote, "We hereby pledge our lives, our fortunes and our sacred honor" to the signing of the Declaration of Independence.

In his book ***Trust: The Social Virtues and the Creation of Prosperity,*** philosopher Francis Fukuyama observed that societies worldwide can be divided into two kinds: "high-trust" and "low-trust." He also argues that the highest-trust societies—those in which integrity is most admired, encouraged, and respected—are also the most law-abiding, free, and prosperous.

At the other end of the societal spectrum, however, are those societies characterized by tyranny, thievery, dishonesty, and corruption. Each of these are, without exception, both undemocratic and poor.

Trust Is the Key. Trust is the lubricant of human relationships. Where there is high trust among and between people, economic activity flourishes and there are opportunities for all. On the other hand, where there is low trust, economic resources are squandered in an attempt to protect against thievery and corruption—or these resources are not available at all.

In the United States, we have the Constitution and Bill of Rights. These documents lay out the rules by which Americans agree to live. They create the structure of our government and guarantee our rights. But they assume that our elected representatives will be men and women of honor, committed to protecting and defending those rights. They attempt to assure that only men and women of character can thrive and prosper over the long term in our economic, political, and social system. They aim to assure that, in most cases, only men and women of character can rise to high positions in society.

Although our system is not perfect, and people of questionable character occasionally rise to positions of prominence, it is seldom for very long. The basic demand of Americans for honesty and integrity eventually leads to the exposure and censure of dishonest people. The demand for men and women of character continues unabated.

Your Self-Image: Your Inner Mirror. The second part of your personality is your ***self-image***. This is the way we see and think about ourselves, especially prior to any event of importance. People always tend to behave on the outside consistently with the way they see themselves on the inside. This is often called our "inner mirror," into which we peer before we engage in any behavior.

When you see yourself as calm, positive, truthful, and possessed of high character, you behave with greater strength and personal power. Other people respect you more. You feel in control of yourself and the situation.

What's more, whenever you actually behave in a manner that is consistent with your highest values, your self-image improves. You see and think about yourself in a better light. You feel happier and more confident. Your behavior and outward performance then reflect this increasingly improving inner picture you have of yourself as the very best person you can possibly be.

People tend to accept you at your own evaluation of yourself, at least initially. If you see and think of yourself as an excellent person who is possessed of high character, you will treat other people with courtesy, grace, and respect. In turn, they will likewise treat you as a person of honor and character.

Your Self-Esteem: How Much You Like Yourself. The third part of your personality is your *self-esteem*. This is how you feel about yourself, your emotional core. Your self-esteem is defined as "how much you like yourself," but it's more than only this. The more you see yourself as a valuable and important person, the more positive and optimistic you will be. When you truly consider yourself to be important and worthwhile, you will treat other people as if they are important as well.

Your self-esteem is largely determined by how consistent your self-image, which shapes your personal behavior, is with your self-ideal, or your vision of the very best person you can possibly be.

Whenever you act consistently with who you consider an excellent person to be, your self-image improves and your self-esteem increases. You like and respect yourself more. You feel happy about yourself and others. The more you like yourself, the more you like others, and the more they like you in return. By acting with character and in harmony with your highest values, you put your entire life (internally and externally) into an upward spiral. In every area of your life, things will get better and better for you.

Your role models have a tremendous impact on shaping your character. The more you admire a person and his or her qualities, the more you strive—both consciously and unconsciously—to become like that person. This is why clarity is so important.

Always Behave Consistently

Whenever you act in a way that is consistent with your values, you feel ***good*** about yourself. Whenever you compromise your values, for any reason, you feel ***bad*** about yourself. This also means that when you compromise your values, your self-confidence and self-esteem go down. You feel uneasy and inferior, inadequate and uncomfortable.

When you compromise your values, deep down inside, you feel that something is fundamentally wrong.

Almost all human problems can be solved by a return to your highest values and your innermost convictions. When you look back, there have probably been situations in your life when you have compromised your values in order to save an investment, keep a job, preserve a relationship, or maintain a friendship. In each case, you have felt worse and worse until you finally broke it off and walked away.

And how did you feel when you finally had the strength of character to walk away? You felt ***wonderful***! Whenever you use your willpower and strength of character to return to the values that are most dear to you, you are rewarded with a wonderful feeling of happiness and exhilaration. You feel energized and free. You wonder why you didn't make that decision a long time ago.

Do the Right Thing

In the development of character that is based on self-discipline and willpower, long-term thinking is essential. The more you think about the long-term consequences of your behavior, the more likely it is that you will do the right thing in the short term. So when you have to make a choice or decision, always ask the magic question, "What's important here?"

Practice the Universal Maxim of Immanuel Kant: "Resolve to behave as though your every act were to become a universal law for all people."

One of the great questions for the development of character is this: "What kind of a world would this world be if everyone in it was just like ***me***?"

Whenever you slip, whenever you do or say something that is inconsistent with your highest values, immediately "get back on your horse." Say to yourself, "This is not like me!" and resolve that next time you will do better.

What You Dwell Upon Grows

If you are in a situation today in which you are not living up to your highest values, make a decision, this very minute, to confront the situation and straighten it out. The minute you do, you will once again feel happy and back in control.

> There is an old Indian story: "On my shoulders are two wolves. One is a black wolf, evil, who continually tempts me to do and say the wrong things. On my other shoulder is a white wolf that continually encourages me to live up to my very best."
>
> A listener asked the old man, "Which of these wolves has the greatest power over you?"
>
> The old man replied, "The one I feed."

By the Law of Concentration, whatever you dwell on grows and increases in your life. When you think and talk about the virtues and values that you most admire and respect, you therefore program those values deeper and deeper into your subconscious until they begin to operate automatically in every situation.

Whenever you exercise your self-discipline
power to live your life consistently with those values th..
you most aspire to be known for, you begin to move rapidly along the path to becoming an excellent person.

Action Exercises:

Take out a sheet of paper and write out your answers to these questions.

1. Name three people, living or dead, who you most admire and describe one quality of each of them that you respect.
2. Determine the most important virtue or quality in your life that you strive the most to practice or emulate.
3. Identify those situations in which you feel the most confident, in which you feel like the very best person you could possibly be.
4. What situations give you your greatest feelings of self-esteem and personal worth?
5. If you were already an excellent person in every respect, how would you behave differently from today onward?
6. What one quality would you like people to think of when your name is mentioned, and what could you do to ensure this happens?
7. In what one area do you need to be more truthful and practice higher levels of integrity than you do today?

Chapter 3

Self-Discipline and Responsibility

"The individual who wants to reach the top in business must appreciate the might and force of habit. He must be quick to break those habits that can break him–and hasten to adopt those practices that will become the habits that help him achieve the success he desires."

—J. PAUL GETTY

Your ability and willingness to discipline yourself to accept personal responsibility for your life are essential to happiness, health, success, achievement, and personal leadership. Accepting responsibility is one of the hardest of all disciplines, but without it, no success is possible.

The failure to accept responsibility and the attempt to foist responsibility for things in your life that make you unhappy onto other people, institutions, and situations completely distort cause and effect, undermine your character, weaken your resolve, and diminish your humanity. They lead to making endless excuses.

MY GREAT REVELATION

When I was twenty-one, I was living in a tiny apartment and working as a construction laborer. I had to get up at

5:00 A.M. so that I could take three buses to work in order to be there by 8:00 A.M. I didn't get home until 7:00 P.M., tired out from carrying construction materials all day. I was making just enough money to get by, and I had no car, almost no savings, and just enough clothes for my needs. I had no radio or television.

It was the middle of a cold winter, with the temperature at minus 35 degrees Fahrenheit, so I seldom went out in the evening. Instead, if I had enough energy, I sat in my small apartment at my little table in my kitchen nook and read.

One evening, late at night, as I was sitting there by myself at the table, it suddenly dawned on me that "this is my life." This life was not a rehearsal for something else. The game was on, and I was the main character, as in a play.

It was like a flashbulb going off in my face. I looked at myself and around me at my small apartment, and I considered the fact that I had not graduated from high school. The only work that I was qualified to do was manual labor. I earned just enough money to pay my basic expenses, and I had very little left over at the end of each month.

I suddenly knew that unless I changed, nothing else was going to change. No one else was going to do it for me. In reality, no one else cared. I realized at that moment that, from that day forward I was completely responsible for my life and for everything that happened to me. *I* was responsible. I could no longer blame my situation on my difficult childhood or mistakes I had made in the past. I was in charge. I was in the driver's seat. This was my life, and if I didn't do something to change it, it would go on like this indefinitely, by the simple force of inertia.

This revelation changed my life. I was never the same again. From that moment on, I accepted more and more responsibility for everything in my life. I accepted responsibility for doing my job better than before rather than doing only the minimum that was necessary to avoid getting fired. I accepted responsibility for my finances, my health, and, especially, my future.

The very next day, I went down to a local bookstore at my lunch break and began the lifelong practice of buying books with information, ideas, and lessons that could help me. I dedicated my life to self-improvement, to continuous learning in every way possible.

For the rest of my business life, right up to the present moment, whenever I've wanted or needed to learn something to help me, I have returned to learning, to reading, to listening to audio programs and attending courses and seminars. I found that you could learn anything you need to learn in order to accomplish any goal you set for yourself.

Over time, I learned that fully 80 percent of the population never accepts complete responsibility for their lives. They continually complain, criticize, make excuses, and blame other people for things in their lives about which they are not happy. The consequences of this way of thinking, however, can be disastrous. They can sabotage all hopes for success and happiness later in life.

From Childhood to Maturity

When you are growing up, from an early age you become conditioned to see yourself as not responsible for your life. This is normal and natural. When you are a child, your parents are in charge. They make all your decisions. They decide what food you will eat, what clothes you will wear, what toys you will play with, what home you will live in, what school you will attend, and what activities you will engage in during your spare time. Because you are young, innocent, and unknowing, you do what they want you to do. You have little choice or control.

As you grow up, however, you begin to make more and more of your own decisions in each of these areas. But because of your early programming, you are conditioned unconsciously to feel that someone else is still responsible for your life, that there is still someone else out there who can or should take care of you.

Most people grow up believing that if something goes wrong, someone else is responsible. Someone else is to blame. Someone else is guilty. Someone else is the villain and they are the victim. As a result, most people make more and more excuses for the things in their lives, past and present, that make them unhappy.

Get Over the Mistakes Your Parents Made

If your parents criticized you or got angry with you for mistakes you made when you were growing up, you began to unconsciously assume that somehow you were at fault. If your parents punished you physically or emotionally for doing or not doing something that pleased or displeased them, you felt inferior and inadequate.

When your parents withheld their love to punish you for not doing something they demanded, you might have grown up with deep feelings of guilt, unworthiness, and undeservingness. All these negative feelings could then intersect to make you feel like a victim, like you were not responsible for yourself or your life once you became an adult.

The most common feeling that we have as adults if we have been raised in a critical home environment is the feeling that "I'm not good enough." Because of this feeling, we compare ourselves unfavorably to others. We think that other people who seem to be happier or more confident are better than us. We develop feelings of inferiority. This can become an emotional trap.

The Fatal Fallacy

If we think for any reason that others are ***better*** than us, we unconsciously assume that we must be ***worse*** than they are. If they are "worth more" than we are, we assume that we must be "worth less." This feeling of inadequacy or worthlessness lies at the root of most personality problems in our lives as well as most political and social problems in our world, both nationally and internationally.

To escape from these feelings of guilt and worthlessness that have been instilled in us as the result of destructive criticism in childhood, we lash out at our world, other people, and situations. In any part of our life with which we are unhappy or discontented, our first reaction is to look around and ask, "Who's to blame?"

Most religions teach the concept of sin, which states that whenever something goes wrong, someone is to blame. Someone has done something bad. Someone is guilty. Someone must be punished. This whole idea of guilt and punishment leads to ever-increasing feelings of anger, resentment, and irresponsibility.

An Attitude of Irresponsibility

Our courts today are clogged with thousands of people demanding redress and payment for something that went wrong in their lives. Backed up by ambitious plaintiff lawyers, people go to court demanding compensation, even if they themselves are completely at fault for what happened—***especially*** if they are at fault.

People don't want to accept responsibility. People spill hot coffee on themselves and sue the fast food restaurant that sold them the coffee in the first place. People get drunk and drive off the road and then turn around and sue the manufacturer of the fifteen-year-old car they were driving. People climb up on a stepladder and lean over too far, falling to the ground. They then sue the ladder manufacturer for their injury. In each case, people are attempting to escape responsibility for their own behaviors by blaming someone else, making excuses, and then demanding compensation.

Eliminating Negative Emotions

The common denominator of all people is the desire to be ***happy***. In its simplest terms, happiness arises from the ***absence*** of negative emotions. Where there are no negative emotions, all that is left is positive emotions. Therefore, the elimination of negative emotions is your great business in life if you truly wish to be happy.

There are dozens of negative emotions. Although the most common are guilt, resentment, envy, jealousy, fear, and hostility, they all ultimately boil down to a feeling of ***anger***, directed either inward or outward.

Anger is directed inwardly when you bottle it up rather than expressing it constructively to others. Anger is directed outwardly when you criticize or attack other people.

Psychosomatic Illness

Negative emotions are the major causes of ***psychosomatic*** illness. This occurs when the mind (***psycho***) makes the body (***soma***) sick. Negative emotions, especially as expressed in the form of anger, weaken your immune system and make you susceptible to colds, flu, and other diseases. Uncontrolled bursts of anger can actually bring about heart attacks, strokes, and nervous breakdowns.

Here is the great discovery: All negative emotions, especially anger, depend for their very existence on your ability to ***blame*** someone or something else for something in your life that you are not happy about.

It takes tremendous self-discipline to refrain from blaming others for our problems. It takes enormous self-control to refuse to make excuses.

It takes tremendous self-discipline for you to accept complete responsibility for everything you are, everything you become, and everything that happens to you. Even if you are not directly responsible for something that happens, like hurricane Katrina, you are responsible for your responses, for what you do and say from that moment forward. It takes tremendous self-mastery for you to take complete control of your conscious mind and deliberately choose to think positive, constructive thoughts that enhance your life and improve the quality of your relationships and results. But the payoff is tremendous.

Blaming Is Easy

By following the path of least resistance, the easiest and most mindless behavior of all is for a person to lash out and blame someone else anytime anything goes wrong, for any reason.

People who develop the habit of automatically blaming often become angry at ***things***. Blaming inanimate objects when they do not function as expected is so silly that it almost becomes a mild form of insanity.

People become angry at doors that stick. They swear at tools they are using when they themselves make a mistake. They get mad when their car doesn't start. Even if it is an inanimate object, if it doesn't work perfectly, then the thing must be to blame. People will often kick a car that they are mad at or a box that they tripped over.

The Antidote to Negative Emotions

The fastest and most dependable way to eliminate negative emotions is to immediately say, "I am responsible!" Whenever something happens that triggers anger or a negative reaction of any kind, quickly neutralize the feelings of negativity by saying, "I am responsible."

The Law of Substitution says that you can substitute a positive thought for a negative one. Since your mind can hold only one thought at a time, when you deliberately choose the positive thought, "I am responsible," you cancel out any other thought or emotion at that moment.

It is not possible to accept responsibility and remain angry at the same time. It is not possible to accept responsibility and experience negative emotions. It is not possible to accept responsibility without becoming calm, clear, positive, and focused once more.

As long as you are blaming someone else for something in your life that you don't like, you will remain a "mental child." You continue to see yourself as small and helpless, like a victim. You continue to lash out. However, when you begin to accept responsibility for everything that happens to you, you transform yourself into a "mental adult." You will see yourself as being in charge of your own life, and no longer a victim.

In Alcoholics Anonymous, people who are having problems with drinking attend meetings with others going through the same situation. What they have found is that until the individual accepts responsibility for his or her problems, both with alcohol and in other areas of life, no progress is possible. But after the person accepts responsibility, everything is possible. This is true with almost every difficult situation in life in which you project your unhappiness onto other people or factors outside yourself.

Money and Emotions

Many of our biggest problems and concerns in life have to do with money: earning it, spending it, investing it, and, especially, losing it. As a result, many of our negative emotions are associated with money in some way. However, the fact is that you are responsible for your financial life. You choose. You decide. You are in charge. You cannot blame your financial problems or situation on other people. You are in the driver's seat.

So it is only when you accept responsibility for your income (who chose to accept the job you are working at?), your bills (who spent the money that put you into debt?), and your investments (who made those decisions?) can you move from being an "economic child" to an "economic adult."

Responsibility and Control

There is a direct relationship between the acceptance of responsibility and the amount of personal control you feel you have over your life. This means that the more you accept responsibility, the greater ***sense of control*** you experience.

There is also a direct relationship between the amount of control you feel you have and how positive you feel. The more you feel that you have a high "sense of control" in the important areas of your life, the more positive and happy you are in everything you do.

When you accept responsibility, you feel strong, powerful, and purposeful. Accepting responsibility eliminates the negative emotions that rob you of happiness and contentment.

In every situation, the antidote to negative emotions is to say, “I am responsible.” Then look into the situation to find the reasons why you are responsible for what happened or for what is going on.

Your intelligence is like a double-edged sword: It can cut in either direction. You can use your intelligence to rationalize, justify, and blame other people for things you are not happy about, or you can use your intelligence to find reasons why you are responsible for what happened and then take action to solve the problem or resolve the situation. You can make excuses or you can make progress. You choose.

Even if an accident has occurred, such as your car being damaged in the parking lot while you are at work, you may not be ***legally*** at fault for the accident. But you are still responsible for your responses, for how you behave as a result of what happened.

Never Complain, Never Explain

The mark of the leader, the truly superior person, is that he or she accepts complete responsibility for the situation. It is not possible to imagine a true leader who whines and complains rather than taking action when problems and difficulties arise.

This sense of “response-ability” is the mark of the highly developed personality: You take responsibility for your life by resolving, in advance, that you will not become upset or angry over something that you cannot affect or change. Just as you do not become angry about the weather, you do not become angry over circumstances and situations over which you have no control.

Furthermore, you especially do not allow yourself to be angry and unhappy in the present because of unhappy experiences or situations from the ***past***. You say, "What cannot be cured must be endured."

It is amazing how many people are unhappy today because of a past event, even something that happened many years ago. Each time they think of the negative experience, they become angry or depressed once again. The good news is that at any time, you can stop thinking about, discussing, and rehashing the past. You can let it go and begin thinking instead about your goals and your unlimited future. As Helen Keller said, "When you turn toward the sunshine, the shadows fall behind you."

Self-Mastery and Self-Control

Any self-discipline, self-mastery, and self-control begin with taking responsibility for your ***emotions***. You take charge of your emotions by accepting 100 percent responsibility for yourself and for your responses to everything that happens to you. You refuse to make excuses, complain, criticize, or blame other people for anything. Instead, you say, "I am responsible," and then take action of some kind.

The Only Antidote Is Action

The only real antidote for anger or worry is purposeful action in the direction of your goals—which is the subject of the next chapter. Before you turn to that, however, resolve today to first take complete control of your thoughts, feeling, and actions, and then to get so busy working on things that are important to you that you don't have time to think about or express negative emotions to or about anyone, for any reason.

When you exert your self-discipline and willpower in the acceptance of personal responsibility for your life, you take complete control of your thoughts and feelings. By doing so, you become a much more effective, happy, and positive person in everything you do.

Action Exercises:

1. Resolve today to accept 100 percent responsibility for everything you are and for everything you become. Never complain, never explain.
2. Look into your past and select a person or incident that still makes you unhappy today. Instead of justifying your negative feelings, look for reasons why ***you*** were partially responsible for what happened.
3. Select a relationship in your past that made you unhappy, and then give three reasons why ***you*** were responsible for what occurred.
4. Select one person in your past with whom you are still angry and resolve to forgive that person completely for what happened. This act will liberate you emotionally.

5. Accept complete responsibility for your financial situation and refuse to blame any financial problems on anyone else. Now, what steps are you going to take to resolve that situation?
6. Accept complete responsibility for your family situation, with each person, and then take immediate action to improve your relationships wherever there may be problems.
7. Accept 100 percent responsibility for your health. Resolve today to do or stop doing whatever is necessary for you to attain excellent all-around health.

Chapter 4

Self-Discipline and Goals

"Discipline is the bridge between goals and accomplishment."
—Jim Rohn

Your ability to discipline yourself to set clear goals for yourself and then to work toward them every day will do more to guarantee your success than any other single factor. You need to have goals to accomplish worthwhile things in life. You have probably heard it said that "you can't hit a target that you can't see."

"If you don't know where you're going, any road will get you there."

And as Wayne Gretsky said, "You miss every shot you don't take."

The very act of taking the time to decide what you really want in each area of your life can change your life completely.

• • •

The 3 Percent Factor

It seems that only 3 percent of adults have written goals and plans, and ***this 3 percent earn more than all of the other 97 percent put together.***

Why is this? The simplest answer is that if you have clear goal and a plan to achieve it, you therefore have a track to run on every single day. Instead of being sidetracked by distractions and diversions, getting lost or going astray, more and more of your time is focused in a straight line—from where you are to where you want to go. This is why people with goals accomplish so much more than people without them.

The tragedy is that most people think that they already have goals. But what they really have are ***hopes*** and ***wishes.*** However, hope is not a strategy for success, and a wish has been defined as a "goal with no energy behind it."

Goals that are not written down and developed into plans are like bullets without powder in the cartridge. People with unwritten goals go through life shooting blanks. Because they think they already have goals, they never engage in the hard, disciplined effort of goal-setting—and this is the master skill of success.

Multiply Your Chances of Success

In 2006, *USA Today* reported a study in which researchers selected a large number people who had made New Year's resolutions. They then divided these people into two categories: those who had set New Year's resolutions and written them down and those who had set New Year's resolutions but had not written them down.

Twelve months later, they followed up on the respondents in this study, and what they found was astonishing. Of the people who had set New Year's resolutions but had ***not*** written them down, ***only 4 percent*** had actually followed through on their resolutions. But among the group who ***had*** written down their New Year's resolutions (an exercise requiring only a couple of minutes), ***44 percent had followed through*** on them. This is a difference of more than 1,100 percent in success, and it was achieved by the simple act of crystallizing the resolutions or goals on paper.

The Discipline of Writing

In my experience of working with several million people over the past twenty-five years, the disciplined act of writing out goals, making plans for accomplishing them, and then working on those goals daily increases the likelihood of achieving your goals by ten times, or 1,000 percent.

This does not mean that writing out your goals ***guarantees*** success, but rather that it increases the ***probability of success*** by ten times. These are very good odds to have working in your favor, especially when there is no cost or risk involved in putting pen to paper—just a little time.

Writing is called a "psycho-neuro-motor activity." The act of writing forces you to think and concentrate. It forces you to choose what is more important to you and your future. As a result, when you write down a goal, you impress it into your subconscious mind, which then goes to work twenty-four hours a day to bring your goal to reality.

Sometimes I tell my seminar audiences, "Only 3 percent of adults have written goals, and everyone else works for those people." In life, you either work to achieve your own goals or you work to achieve the goals of someone else. Which is it going to be?

Success Versus Failure Mechanisms

Your brain has both a success mechanism and a failure mechanism. The failure mechanism is the temptation to follow the undisciplined path of least resistance, to do what is fun and easy rather than what is hard and necessary. Your failure mechanism operates automatically throughout your life, which is the major reason why most people fail to fulfill their individual potentials.

While your failure mechanism functions automatically, your success mechanism is triggered by a goal. When you decide on a goal, you override your failure mechanism, and can you change the direction of your life. You go from being a ship without a rudder, drifting with the tide, to being a ship with a rudder, a compass, and a clear destination, sailing in a straight direction toward your goal.

The Power of Goals

A client of mine recently told me an interesting story. He said he had attended one of my seminars in 1994, where I spoke about the importance of writing down goals and making plans for accomplishing them. At that time, he was thirty-five years old, selling cars for a dealership in Nashville, and earning about $50,000 a year.

He told me that day changed his life. He began writing out his goals and plans and working on them daily. Twelve years later, he was earning more than $1 million a year and was the president of a fast-growing company that sells services to some of the biggest companies in the country. He told me he could not imagine what his life would have been like if he had not taken out a piece of paper and written down the goals he wanted to achieve in the years ahead.

Take Control of Your Life

Aristotle wrote that human beings are ***teleological*** organisms, which simply means that we are ***purpose driven***. Therefore, you feel happy and in control of your life only when you have a clear goal that you are working toward each day. This also means that this ability to become a lifelong goal setter is one of the most important disciplines you will ever develop.

In nature, the homing pigeon is a remarkable bird. It has an uncanny instinct that enables it to fly back to its home roost, no matter how far away it starts or in what direction it must go. You can take a homing pigeon out of its roost, put it in a cage, put the cage in a box, cover the box with a blanket, and put the covered box in the back of a pickup truck. You could then drive 1,000 miles in any direction, open up the truck, take out the box, take off the blanket, open the cage, and throw the homing pigeon up into the air.

The homing pigeon will circle three times, get its bearings, and then fly straight back to its home roost. This is the only creature on earth that has this ability—except for human beings. Except for ***you.***

You also have this remarkable homing ability within your own brain, but with one special difference. The homing pigeon seems to know ***instinctively*** exactly where its home roost is located. It then has the ability to fly directly back to that roost. In contrast, when human beings program a goal into their minds, they can then set out without having ***any idea*** where they will go or how they will achieve that goal. But by some miracle, they will begin to move unerringly toward that goal, and the goal will begin to move toward them.

Still, many people are hesitant to set goals. They say, "I want to be financially independent, but I have no idea how I'm going to get there." As a result, they don't even set financial success as a goal. But the good news is that ***you don't need to know how to get there.*** You just need to be clear about what you want to accomplish, and the goal-striving mechanism in your brain will guide you unerringly to your destination.

For example, you can decide that you are going to find your ideal job, in which you work for and with people you like and respect and do work that is both challenging and enjoyable. You take some time to write down an exact description of what your ideal job and workplace would look like, and then you go out into the job market and begin searching.

After a series of interviews, you will often walk into the right place at the right time and find yourself in exactly the right job. Almost everyone has had this experience at one time or another. You can have it by ***design*** rather than by chance simply by developing absolute clarity about what you really want.

The Seven-Step Method to Achieving Your Goals

There are seven simple steps that you can follow to set and achieve your goals faster. There are more complex and detailed goal-achieving methodologies, but this Seven-Step Method will enable you to accomplish ten times more than you have ever accomplished before, and you will do so far faster than you can currently imagine.

Step 1: Decide* Exactly *What You Want. Be specific. If you want to increase your income, decide on a specific amount of money rather than to just "make more money."

Step 2: Write It Down. A goal that is not in writing is like cigarette smoke: It drifts away and disappears. It is vague and insubstantial. It has no force, effect, or power. But a written goal becomes something that you can see, touch, read, and modify if necessary.

Step 3: Set a Deadline for Your Goal. Pick a reasonable time period and write down the date when you want to achieve it. If it is a big enough goal, set a final deadline and then set subdeadlines or interim steps between where you are today and where you want to be in the future.

A deadline serves as a "forcing system" in your brain. Just as you often get more done when you are under the pressure of a specific deadline, your subconscious mind works faster and more efficiently when you have decided that you want to achieve a goal by a specific time.

The rule is "There are no unrealistic goals; there are only unrealistic deadlines."

What do you do if you don't achieve your goal by your deadline? Simple. You set another deadline. A deadline is just a "guesstimate." Sometimes you will achieve your goal before the deadline, sometimes at the deadline, and sometimes after the deadline.

When you set your goal, it will be within the context of a certain set of external circumstances. But these circumstances may change, causing you to change your deadline as well.

Step 4: Make a List of* Everything *You Can Think of That You Could Possibly Do to Achieve Your Goal. As Henry Ford said, "The biggest goal can be accomplished if you just break it down into enough small steps."

- Make a list of the ***obstacles and difficulties*** that you will have to overcome, both external and internal, in order to achieve your goal.
- Make a list of the additional ***knowledge and skills*** that you will need in order to achieve your goal.
- Make a list of the ***people*** whose cooperation and support you will require to achieve your goal.

- Make a list of everything that you can think of that you will have to do, and then add to this list as new tasks and responsibilities occur to you. Keep writing until your list is complete.

Step 5: Organize Your List by Both Sequence and Priority. A list of activities organized by ***sequence*** requires that you decide what you need to do first, what you need to do second, and what you need to do later on. In addition, a list organized by ***priority*** enables you to determine what is more important and what is less important.

Sometimes sequence and priority are the same, but often they are not. For example, if you want to start a particular kind of business, the first item in order of sequence might be for you to purchase a book or enroll in a course on that business.

But what is most important is your ability to develop a business plan, based on complete market research, that you can use to gather the resources you need and actually start the business you have in mind.

Step 6: Take Action on Your Plan Immediately. Take the first step—and then the second step and the third step. Get going. Get busy. Move quickly. Don't delay. Remember: Procrastination is not only the thief of time; it is the thief of life.

The difference between successes and failures in life is simply that winners take the ***first step***. They are action-oriented. As they said in *Star Trek*, they "go boldly where no man has ever gone before." Winners are willing to take action with no guarantees of success. Though they're willing to face failure and disappointment, they're always willing to take action.

Step 7: Do Something **Every Day** ***That Moves You in the Direction of Your Major Goal.*** This is the key step that will guarantee your success: Do something, seven days a week, 365 days a year. Do ***anything*** that moves you at least one step closer to the goal that is most important to you at that time.

When you do something every day that moves you in the direction of your goal, you develop ***momentum***. This momentum, this sense of forward motion, motivates, inspires, and energizes you. As you develop momentum, you will find it increasingly easy to take even more steps toward your goal.

In no time at all, you will have developed the discipline of setting and achieving your goals. It will soon become easy and automatic. You will soon develop the habit and the discipline of working toward your goals all the time.

The Ten-Goal Exercise

This is one of the most powerful goal-achieving methods I have ever discovered. I teach it all over the world, and I practice it myself almost every day.

Take out a clean sheet of paper. At the top of the page write the word "Goals" and today's date. Then, discipline yourself to write down ten goals that you'd like to accomplish in the next twelve months. Write down financial, family goals, and fitness goals, as well as goals for personal possessions, like a house or a car.

Don't worry for the moment about how you are going to achieve these goals. Just write them down as quickly as you can. You can write as many as fifteen goals if you like, but this exercise requires that you write down a minimum of ten within three to five minutes.

Select One Goal

Once you have written out your ten goals, imagine for the moment that you can achieve all of the goals on your list if you want them long enough and hard enough. Also imagine that you have a "magic wand" that you can wave that will enable you to achieve any ***one*** goal on your list within twenty-four hours.

If you could achieve any one goal on your list within twenty-four hours, which one would have the ***greatest positive impact*** on your life right now? Which one goal would change or improve your life more than anything else? Which one goal, if you were to achieve it, would help you to achieve more of your other goals than anything else?

Whatever your answer to this question, put a circle around this goal and then write it at the top of a clean sheet of paper. This goal then becomes your "Major Definite Purpose." It becomes your focal point and the organizing principle of your future activities.

• • •

Make a Plan

Once you have written out this goal, clearly and specifically, and made it measurable, set a deadline on your goal. Your subconscious mind needs a deadline so that it can focus and concentrate all your mental powers on goal attainment.

Make a list of everything that you can think of that you could do to achieve your goal. Organize this list by sequence and priority.

Select the most important or logical next step in your plan and take action on it immediately. Take the first step. Do ***something***. Do ***anything***.

Resolve to work on this goal every single day until it is achieved. From this moment forward, as far as you are concerned, "Failure is not an option." Once you have decided that this one goal can have the greatest positive impact on your life and you have set it as your major definite purpose, resolve that you will work toward this goal as hard as you can, as long as you can, and that you will never give up until it is achieved. This decision alone can change your life.

Use "Mindstorming" to Get Started

Here is another technique you can use to dramatically increase the likelihood that you will achieve your most important goal. This is the most powerful creative thinking technique I have ever seen. More people have become wealthy using this method than any other way.

Take another clean sheet of paper. Write out your Major Definite Purpose at the top of the page in the form of a ***question***. Then discipline yourself to write a minimum of twenty answers to the question.

For example, if your goal is to earn a certain amount of money by a certain date, you would write the question as, "How can I earn $XXX by this specific date?"

You then discipline yourself to generate twenty answers to your question. This exercise of "mindstorming" will activate your mind, unleash your creativity, and give you ideas that you may never have thought of before.

The first three to five answers will be easy. The next five will be difficult, and the last ten answers will be harder than you can imagine, at least the first time you do this exercise. Nonetheless, you must exert your discipline and willpower to persist until you have written down at least twenty answers.

Once you have generated twenty answers, look over your list and select one of those answers to take action on immediately. It seems that when you take action on a single idea on your list, it triggers more ideas and motivates you to take action on even more of these answers.

The Great Law of Cause and Effect

The most important application of the law of cause and effect is that "thoughts are causes, and conditions are effects."

Your thoughts create the conditions of your life. When you change your thinking, you change your life. Your outer world becomes a mirror-image reflection of your inner world.

Perhaps the greatest discovery in the history of thought is that "you become what you think about most of the time." Moreover, the teacher John Boyle said, "Whatever you can think about on a continuing basis, you can have."

Napoleon Hill, author of the success classic ***Think and Grow Rich***—which was first published in 1939 and is still selling today—said, "Whatever the mind of man can conceive and believe, it can achieve."

When you think about your goal continually and work on it every day, more and more of your mental resources will be concentrated on moving you toward that goal—and moving your goal toward you.

The discipline of daily goal-setting will make you a powerful, purposeful, and irresistible person. You will develop self-esteem, self-confidence, and self-respect. As you feel yourself moving toward your goals faster and faster, you will ultimately become unstoppable.

In the next chapter, I will explain how the use of self-discipline to develop personal excellence is the most powerful step you can take to achieve all your material and emotional goals.

Action Exercises:

1. Resolve today to "switch on" your success mechanism and unlock your goal-achieving mechanism by deciding exactly what you ***really*** want in life.

2. Make a list of ten goals that you want to achieve in the foreseeable future. Write them down in the present tense, as if you have already achieved them.
3. Select the one goal that could have the greatest positive impact on your life if you were to achieve it, and write it down at the top of another piece of paper.
4. Make a list of everything you could do to achieve this goal, organize it by sequence and priority, and then take action on it immediately.
5. Practice mindstorming by writing out twenty ideas that could help you achieve your most important goal, and then take action on at least one of those ideas.
6. Resolve to do something every day, seven days a week, to achieve your most important goal until you are successful.
7. Continually remind yourself that "failure is not an option." No matter what, resolve to persist until you succeed.

Chapter 5

Self-Discipline and Personal Excellence

"We are what we repeatedly do; excellence then is not an act but a habit."
—Aristotle

You are your most valuable asset. Your life, your potential, and your possibilities are the most precious things you have. Thus your great goal in life should be to fulfill that potential and become everything you are capable of becoming.

Your ability to learn, grow, and fulfill your potential is unlimited. Today, people are graduating from high school and college in their seventies, learning new subjects and developing new capabilities. Your ability to learn and remember can continue throughout your life if you keep your brain alive, alert, and functioning at its best.

Your most precious financial asset is your ***earning ability***. Your ability to work is your primary source of cash throughout your life. You could lose your home, your car, your bank account, and everything you own, but as long as you have your earning ability, you can earn it all back—and more—in the months and years ahead.

Your Biggest Investment

Most people don't realize this. They take their earning ability for granted. But it has taken you your entire life to develop your earning ability. Every bit of education, experience, and hard work that you have invested in learning your craft and developing your skills has gone into building this asset.

Your earning ability is very much like a muscle. It can increase in strength and power year by year as the result of regular exercise. Likewise, the opposite is true, too: If left alone or ignored, your earning ability, like your muscles, can become weaker or even decline because you have simply failed to upgrade it continually.

In other words, your earning ability can be either an ***appreciating*** or a ***depreciating*** asset. An appreciating asset is something that grows in value and cash flow every year as the result of continual investment and improvement. A depreciating asset, on the other hand, is something that loses value over time and finally reaches the point at which it is "written off," being of little or no further value. The choice is yours as to whether your earning ability is increasing or decreasing month by month and year by year.

You Are the President

See yourself as the president of your own "Personal Services Corporation." Imagine that you were going to take your company public on the stock market. Would you recommend your company as a ***growth*** stock, continually increasing its value and earning ability each year?

Or would you describe your company as one that has leveled off in the market place, that is not really going anywhere in terms of increased value and income? Would you recommend stock in "You, Inc." as an excellent investment? Why or why not?

What Got You Here Won't Get You Any Further

Some people are actually losing value each year, declining in earning ability, because they are not continually upgrading their knowledge and skills. They don't realize that whatever knowledge and skill they have today is rapidly becoming obsolete. It is being replaced by new knowledge and skills that, if you don't have them and someone else does, you will be in danger of being overtaken by your competition.

Join the Top 20 Percent

In Chapter 1, I mentioned that the 80/20 rule applies to income: The top 20 percent of people in our society earn and control 80 percent of the assets. According to

Forbes, Fortune, Business Week, the ***Wall Street Journal,*** and the IRS, by many estimates the top 1 percent of Americans control as much as 33 percent of the assets.

The most interesting discovery in income inequality is that most millionaires, multimillionaires, and billionaires in America are ***first*** generation. They started with little or nothing and earned all their money by themselves in one lifetime.

In America, there is a high level of income mobility, which means you are able to move from the lower levels of income to the upper levels. Almost everyone who is in the top 20 percent today started in the bottom 20 percent. From that point, they began to do something different with their time and their lives, and as a result, they put themselves squarely onto the upward escalator of financial success.

No Limits on Your Potential

The average income increase in America is about 3 percent a year, just about the same as the rate of inflation and cost of living increases. People whose income is increasing at 3 percent a year seldom get ahead. They have a ***job***, which can also be thought of as an acronym for "*J*ust *O*ver *B*roke."

But the fact is that no one is better than you, and no one is smarter than you. If someone is doing better than you are today, it is simply proof that he has learned how the Law of Cause and Effect applies to his work, and he has begun doing the things that other successful people have also done. The application of the Law of Cause and Effect to your personal life is "learn and do."

The achievement of personal excellence is a decision you make—or that you fail to make. But in the absence of a commitment to excellence in your chosen field, you automatically default to average performance—or even mediocrity. No one becomes excellent accidentally or by just going to work each day. Excellence requires a definite decision and a lifelong commitment.

The Keys to the Twenty-First Century

Knowledge and skill are the keys to the twenty-first century. Becoming the best person you can possibly be and moving to the top of your field require the application of self-discipline throughout your life. Mental fitness is like physical fitness: If you want to achieve either, you must work at it all your life. You can never let up. You must be continually learning and growing—every day, week, and month—throughout your career (and in other areas of your life) if you're going to join the top 20 percent and stay there. To earn more, you must ***learn*** more.

Abraham Lincoln once wrote, "The fact that some have become wealthy is proof that others may do it as well."

What others have done, you can do as well—if you learn ***how***. Everyone who is at the top was once at the bottom. Many people who come from average or poor families with average incomes or who grow up in average circumstances have gone on to become some of the most prominent people in their fields. And what hundreds of thousands and even millions of other people have done, you can do as well. The philosopher Bertrand Russell once wrote that "the very best proof that something can be done is that someone else has already done it."

Ordinary into Extraordinary

Very often, you see people who don't seem to be as intelligent or as talented as you are who are nonetheless accomplishing remarkable things with their lives. There is nothing that will make you angrier than to see someone who seems to be ***dumber*** than you doing better than you. How can this be?

The answer is simple: At a certain point in their lives, they realized that the key to success was personal and professional growth. It was a dedication to lifelong learning.

The good news is that almost every important skill is ***learnable***. Every business skill is learnable. Everyone who is proficient in any area of business was at one time completely ignorant in that area. Every sales skill is learnable. Every top salesperson was once a beginning salesperson and unable to make a call or close a sale. All moneymaking skills are learnable as well. Almost every wealthy person was once poor. You can learn anything you need to learn to achieve any goal you can set for yourself.

Make a Decision

The starting point of your moving upward and onward toward becoming one of the most competent, most respected, and highest paid people in your field is simple: ***Make a decision!***

It is said that every major change in your life comes about when your mind collides with a new idea, and you then make a decision to do something different. You make a decision to complete your education, upgrade your skills, or get into a good college. You make a decision to start a new business. You make a decision to take a particular job or start a particular career. You make a decision to invest your money in a particular way. And, especially, you make a decision to be the best in your field.

Many people say that they would like to be ***happy, healthy, thin,*** and ***rich.*** But (as discussed in Chapter 4), ***wishing*** and ***hoping*** are not enough. You have to make a firm, unequivocal decision that you are going to pay any price and go any distance in order to achieve the goals you have set for yourself. You have to make that decision and then burn your mental bridges behind you. From that minute on, you resolve to continue working on yourself and your craft until you reach the top 20 percent—or beyond.

Follow the Leaders, Not the Followers

When you decide to be one of the best people in your field, look around you and identify the people who are already at the top:

- What characteristics do they have in common?
- How do they plan and organize their days?

- How do they dress?
- How do they walk, talk, and behave with other people?
- What books do they read?
- How do they spend their spare time?
- Who do they associate with?
- What courses have they taken?
- What audio programs do they listen to in their cars?

These are just a few of the questions you should ask in order to find out what successful people are doing that you might also need to do. After all, you can't hit a target that you can't see.

Your selection of the right role models can have an enormous impact on your future. Dr. David MacLelland of Harvard and author of ***The Achieving Society*** concluded that your choice of a "reference group" can determine as much as 95 percent of your success and achievement in life. Your reference group is made of the people who you feel are "just like me." Your natural tendency is to adopt the attitudes, styles of dress, opinions, and lifestyles of the people with whom you identify and associate most of the time.

FLY WITH THE EAGLES

Some years ago, one of my seminar participants told me his story. Bob Barton said he had started off in his twenties in a large company with about thirty-two salespeople in his branch. It was his first real job, and he was starting at the bottom. Because he was new, he hung around with the other junior salespeople. As they say, "Birds of a feather flock together."

After a month or two, Bob noticed that the top salespeople in the office also associated with each other. They did not spend time with the junior salespeople. They also spent their time ***differently***. When Bob got into work in the morning, the top salespeople were already there, planning their days and working on the telephone and making appointments. Bob also noticed that the junior salespeople would come in later, drink coffee, read the newspaper, and make excuses for not making sales calls.

Learn from the Best

Bob decided he was going to pattern himself after the top salespeople in the office. He looked at the way they dressed and groomed, and he resolved to dress and groom the way they did. Each morning, he would stand in front of his mirror and ask himself, "Do I look like one of the top salespeople in my office?"

If the answer was "no," he would go back and change his clothes until he felt that he looked as good as the best people. He began to come into the office and organize his day before 8:30 A.M. so that he was ready to make calls as soon as his customers were available to see him.

One day, Bob asked one of the top salespeople if he could recommend a book or audio program that would help him. It turns out that top people are always willing to help other people improve. When he got the recommendation, Bob immediately went out and got the book and sent away for the audio program. He read the book and listened to the program and then reported back to the top salesman. The top salesman gave him some more advice on things to read and listen to, all of which Bob followed.

Do What the Top People Do

Bob asked another salesperson how he planned his day, and that salesperson showed him his time management system. So Bob began to plan and organize his day the way the top salespeople did it. By using these top salespeople as his role models and emulating them whenever possible, Bob started to make more appointments, see more prospects, and make more sales. Within six months, he was one of the top salespeople in the office as well.

By that time, the top salespeople had invited him for coffee and lunch, and he became one of them, rather than one of the junior people. The next year, Bob went to the national sales conference, where he met a lot of the top people from around the country. He deliberately sought them out and asked for their advice: What books would they suggest? What audio programs would they recommend? What seminars had they attended? What strategies did they find that were the most effective in building their sales business?

Follow the Advice You Get

Bob did something that few people ever do: When he received advice, he ***followed*** it. He immediately took action on the advice and then reported back to the people who had given it to him.

Within four years, Bob became one of the top salespeople in the country. His friends and associates were the other top salespeople in his branch and in the other branches. His income had increased several times. He wore beautiful clothes, drove a new car, lived in a lovely home, and had a wonderful wife. And he said that it all came about as a result of asking top people for their input and then following that input and applying it to his sales activities.

But here's the kicker: Over and over, the top people, the ones who had been winning the sales awards year after year, told Bob the same thing: He was the first person who had ever come up to them and asked them for advice. No one else had ever sought them out and asked them why they were so successful.

The Answers Have All Been Found

Here is a great discovery: All the answers have been found. All the routes to success have been discovered. Everything that you need to learn to move to the top of your field has already been learned by hundreds and even thousands of other people. And if you ask them for advice, they will give it to you. Successful people will have their phone calls held, cancel other appointments, and put their work aside to help other people be successful. But ***you must ask***, and then you must ***follow their advice*** once they give it to you.

If you can't ask them directly, read their books and attend their talks and seminars. Listen to audio programs created by successful people. Sometimes you can send them e-mails and ask for advice. Learn from the best.

Set High Income as a Goal

If your goal is to be in the top 20 percent of money-makers in your field, the first thing you need to do is find out what the people in the top 20 percent are earning today. This information is available. Just ask around. Check industry statistics. Go onto Google. You can find this information if you look for it.

Once you know the income target at which you are aiming, write it down as your goal. Make a plan to achieve this level of income, and work on it every day. Never stop until you reach it.

The secret to high income in business and sales is quite simple: ***learn and do***. Like jacking up a car, you improve one notch at a time. Each time you learn and practice a new skill, you ratchet up your earning ability—and it locks in. As long as you keep increasing your earning ability, you keep ratcheting up to a higher level, from which you seldom decline.

Use the 3 Percent Formula to Invest in Yourself

To guarantee your lifelong success, make a decision today to invest 3 percent of your income back into yourself. This seems to be the magic number for lifelong learning. According to the American Society for Training and Development, this is the percentage that the most profitable 20 percent of companies in every industry invest in the training and development of their staff. Decide today to invest 3 percent of your income into yourself in order to make yourself an appreciating asset, to continually increase your earning ability.

If your annual income goal is $50,000, resolve to invest 3 percent of that amount, or $1,500, back into yourself each year to maintain and upgrade your knowledge and skills. If your income *goal* is $100,000, resolve to invest $3,000 per year back into yourself to ensure that you reach that level of income.

The Payoff Is Extraordinary

I was giving a seminar in Detroit a couple of years ago when a young man, about thirty years old, came up to me at the break. He told me that he had first come to my seminar and heard my "3 Percent Rule" about ten years ago. At that time, he had dropped out of college, was living at home, driving an old car, and earning about $20,000 a year as an office-to-office salesman.

He decided after the seminar that he was going to apply the 3 Percent Rule to himself, and he did so immediately. He calculated 3 percent of his income of $20,000 would be $600. He began to buy sales books and read them every day. He invested in two audio-learning programs on sales and time management. He took one sales seminar. He invested the entire $600 in himself, in learning to become better.

That year, his income went from $20,000 to $30,000, an increase of 50 percent. He said he could trace the increase with great accuracy to the things he had learned and applied from the books he had read and the audio programs he had listened to. So the following year, he invested 3 percent of $30,000, a total of $900, back into himself. That year, his income jumped from $30,000 to $50,000. He began to think, "If my income goes up at 50 percent per year by investing 3 percent back into myself, what would happen if I invested 5 percent?

Keep Raising the Bar

The next year, he invested 5 percent of his income, $2,500, into his learning program. He took more seminars, traveled cross-country to a conference, bought more audio- and video-learning programs, and even hired a part-time coach. And that year, his income ***doubled*** to $100,000.

After that, like playing Texas Hold-Em, he decided to go "all in" and raise his investment into himself to 10 percent per year. He told me that he had been doing this every since.

I asked him, "How has investing 10 percent of your income back into yourself affected your income?"

He smiled and said, "I passed a million dollars in personal income last year. And I still invest 10 percent of my income in myself every single year."

I said, "That's a lot of money. How do you manage to spend that much money on personal development?"

He said, "It's hard! I have to start spending money on myself in January in order to invest it all by the end of the year. I have an image coach, a sales coach, and a speaking coach. I have a large library in my home with every book, audio program, and video program on sales and personal success I can find. I attend conferences, both nationally and internationally in my field. And my income keeps going up and up every year."

Three Simple Steps to Become the Best

Becoming one of the top people in your field requires discipline and application more than anything else. There are three simple steps that you can follow to become the very best in your field:

1. ***Read sixty minutes in your field each day.*** Turn off the television and the radio, put aside the newspaper, and read material about your field for one hour each day before you start working.
2. ***Listen to educational audio programs in your car.*** Start them and stop them as you listen, so you can ***reflect*** on what you have just heard and ***think*** about how you can apply the ideas to your work.
3. ***Attend courses and seminars in your field regularly.*** Seek them out. Take online courses in the

convenience of your own home, courses that enable you to upgrade your skills and give you important ideas that you can use to be even more successful.

The power of compound learning, like compound interest, is quite amazing. The more you learn, the more you *can* learn. The more you learn, the better your brain functions, and the smarter you get. Your memory and retention rate improve. The more you learn, the more relationships you find between something you learned at one time and something you learn at another time.

Never stop learning and growing.

The Achievement of Mastery

How long does it take to achieve mastery in your field? According to the experts, the acquisition of "mastery" requires about seven years, or 10,000 hours of hard work. It takes seven years to become a master salesperson. It takes seven years to become a successful businessperson. It takes seven years to become an excellent diesel mechanic. It takes seven years to become an excellent brain surgeon. It seems to take seven years, or 10,000 hours of hard work, to get to the top of any field. So you might as well get started. The time is going to pass anyway.

The starting point of your achieving mastery is for you to ***commit to excellence***. I have never met a person who made a decision to get into the top 20 percent in their field who did not eventually achieve it. And I never met a person who got there having ***not*** made that decision. Making the decision and then following it up with continuous, purposeful, disciplined action is essential.

Talent Is Not Enough

As I mentioned earlier, according to Geoffrey Colvin in his bestselling book, ***Talent Is Overrated,*** most people learn how to do their job in the first year, and then they never get any better. They just coast in their jobs. But the only direction you can coast is ***downhill.***

Many people will work away at a job for many years and never rise above the average. They will do their job from eight to five, but they never lift a finger to upgrade their skills. They will not invest any time learning their craft unless their company pays for the extra training and gives them the time off to take it.

The average person does only an average job, and as a result, he earns an average income and worries about money all his life. He never realizes that often there is only a thin veil that separates the average person from the excellent person. The fact is that "if you're not getting better, you're getting worse." No one stays in the same place for long.

Two Hours Each Day Will Get You to the Top

It has been calculated that all you need to invest is about two *extra hours* per day to move from the average to the superior. Only two extra hours each day will move you from worrying about money all your life to being one of the highest paid people in your field.

People immediately ask, "Where am I going to get an extra two hours each day?"

It's simple: Take a piece of paper and do the following simple calculation:

- Calculate the number of hours in a week: 7 days times 24 hours equals 168 hours.
- If you deduct forty hours for work and fifty-six hours for sleep, you have seventy-two hours left over.
- If you deduct three hours per day (twenty-one hours) for getting ready for and traveling to and from work, that leaves you fifty-one hours of spare time to do with as you please.
- If you invest two hours per day back into yourself, fourteen hours per week, you still have thirty-seven hours left over. That's an average of more than five hours per day of free time.

All you need to do is devote two hours each day to move you from average performance to superior performance at whatever you choose to do.

Form the Habit of Continuous Learning

The best news is that when you begin reading personal or professional development literature, listening to audio programs in your car, taking additional courses, and upgrading your skills in the evenings and on the weekends rather than watching television, you soon get into the habit of continuous learning. In no time at all, it will become automatic and easy for you to learn, grow, and upgrade your skills every day and every week.

The average adult watches about five hours of television each day. For some people, it is seven or eight hours. They turn on the television first thing in the morning and watch it until they leave for work. They turn it back on as soon as they get home from work. They then watch television until 11 or 12 o'clock at night, going to bed without enough time to get a good night's sleep. They then get up in the morning, drink coffee, and watch television for as long as they can before they go off to work once more.

You Can Be Rich or Poor: It's Your Decision

Your television set can make you rich or poor. If you watch it all the time, it will make you poor. Psychologists have shown that the more television you watch, the lower are your levels of energy and self-esteem. At an unconscious level, you don't like or respect yourself as much if you sit there hour after hour watching television. People who watch too much television also gain weight and become physically unfit from sitting around too much.

Your television can also make you *rich*—but only if you turn it off. When you turn off your television, you free up time that you can then *use* to invest in becoming a better, smarter, and more competent person. When you leave your television off when you are with your family, you will find yourself talking, sharing, communicating, and laughing more often. When you leave your television off for extended periods of time, you break the habit of watching television—and you will hardly miss it at all. Your television can be an excellent servant, but it's a terrible master. The choice is yours.

Increase Your Income 1,000 Percent

There is a simple seven-step formula you can use in order to increase your productivity, performance, output, and income by 1,000 percent over the next ten years. It works for everyone who tries it. It is simple:

First, answer this question: Is it possible for you to increase your overall productivity, performance, and output by 1/10 of 1 percent (1/1000th) in an entire working day? Your answer will probably be "yes." If you were to manage your time a little better, and work on more valuable tasks, you would quite easily increase your output by 1/1000th in a day.

Having done this for the first day, could you increase your output by 1/10 of 1 percent the second day? And the answer, of course, is "yes."

Having increased your performance by 1/10 of 1 percent on Monday and Tuesday, could you continue to do it for Wednesday, Thursday, and Friday? And again, the answer is "yes."

• • •

One Half of 1 Percent Per Week

One tenth of 1 percent times five days per week equals one half of 1 percent per week. Is it possible for a normal, intelligent, hard-working individual to increase his or her output by one half of 1 percent (1/200th) in a single week? Of course it is!

Having done this for the first week, could you keep up the same pace of personal improvement the second week? Of course you could!

Could you get one one-thousandth of 1 percent better five days a week for an entire month? If you could, this means that you would be one half of 1 percent better per week multiplied times four, or 2 percent more productive in an entire month.

There are thirteen four-week months in a year (4 × 13 = 52). Having become 2 percent better in a month, could you repeat that in the second month? In the third month? The fourth month? And so on?

26 Percent Better Each Year

Of course you could! By working on yourself a little bit each day—learning new skills, getting better at your key tasks, setting priorities, and focusing on higher-value activities—you can become 26 percent more productive over the course of an entire year.

Having achieved this goal for the first year, could you do it for the second year, and then the third? Could you keep it up for ten years? And the answer, of course, is yes. And the best news is that when you continue to work on yourself, it becomes easier and easier for you to get better and better as the weeks and months go by.

By the Law of Accumulation, or the Law of Incremental Improvement, by the end of twelve months, you would be 26 percent better. If you continued to improve at 26 percent per year, by the end of ten years, with compounding, you would be 1,004 percent more productive. Your income would increase at the same rate. This formula works—if you do.

Seven Steps to the Top

Here are the seven steps in the 1,000 percent formula:

Step 1: Arise Two Hours Before Your First Appointment, or before you have to be at work. Invest the first hour in yourself by ***reading*** something educational, motivational, or spiritual. As Henry Ward Beecher once said, "The first hour is the rudder of the day."

When you get up and invest the first hour in yourself, you set yourself up mentally to have an excellent day. You will be more positive, alert, creative, and productive all day long when you start your day by investing the first hour in yourself.

If you read in your field one hour per day, that will translate into about one book per week. One book per week will translate into about fifty books per year. Since the average adult reads less than one nonfiction book per year, if you were to read fifty books in your field each year, do you think that would give you an edge in your profession? Do you think that it would move you ahead of virtually everyone else in your business? Of course it would!

If you read fifty books per year for ten years, this would be 500 books that would help you improve your productivity, performance, and income. At the very least, you would need a bigger house just to hold your books. And you would be able to afford it!

Reading one hour per day in your field will make you a national authority in three to five years. This alone can give you your 1,000 percent increase over the course of your career.

Step 2: Rewrite Your Goals, Every Day. Get a spiral notebook and rewrite your major goals in the present tense every morning before you start out, without looking back at what you wrote the previous day. This writing and rewriting is the process of programming instructions into the guidance mechanism of your mind.

When you rewrite your ten goals each morning, you will continually see and think of opportunities to achieve those goals all day long. You will become more focused, channeled, and directed. You will be more purposeful and determined. And you will achieve your goals much faster than if they were merely ***wishes*** floating around in the back of your mind.

Writing and rewriting your goals each day can give you your 1,000 percent increase in income over ten years.

Step 3: Plan Every Day in Advance. Make a list, and set priorities on your work before you start off. Your ability to set priorities and to choose the most important thing that you can be doing at every moment is the key to organizing your life and doubling your productivity. (We will talk in detail about time management techniques in Chapter 12.)

Working on your top priorities can increase your income by 1,000 percent over ten years, and it is probably impossible to achieve without it.

Step 4: Discipline Yourself to Concentrate Single-Mindedly on One Thing. Choose the most important thing that you can do each day. Then, start on it first thing and then work on it until it is 100 percent complete. Your ability to focus and concentrate, when you develop and hone it into a habit, all by itself, will enable you to ***double*** your productivity, performance, and output in the next month—and it will give you your 1,000 percent increase over ten years.

Step 5: Listen to Educational Audio Programs in Your Car. The average businessperson who drives spends 500–1000 hours per year behind the wheel of a car. When you turn your car into a "university on wheels" or a "mobile classroom," you get the educational equivalent of one to two full-time university semesters as you drive around.

Many people have gone from rags to riches by simply listening to educational audio programs in their cars as they drive from place to place. You could do the same. This alone could give you your 1000 percent increase.

Step 6: Ask Two Magic Questions After Every Call or Event. First, ask yourself, "What did I do ***right***?" Then, ask yourself, "What would I do ***differently***?"

The first question, "What did I do ***right***?" forces you to think through and recall all the correct things that you did in that last meeting, presentation, or event, even if it was not successful. Write them down.

The second question, "What would I do ***differently***?" forces you to think through all the different ways you could ***improve*** your performance in a similar situation. Write these ideas down as well.

In both cases, by reviewing your performance, by thinking about what you did ***right*** and what you would do ***differently***, you program yourself to perform even better the next time. This is one of the fastest and most powerful exercises in personal growth and development I have ever discovered. This process dramatically speeds up the rate at which you move into the top 20 percent.

Step 7: Treat Every Person You Meet Like a Million-Dollar Customer. Treat each person you meet and work with, both at home and in the office, as though he or she is the most important person in thc world. When you treat people as if they are valuable and important, they will return the favor by treating you as if ***you*** are valuable and important as well. They will want to be associated with you, work for you, buy from you, and introduce you to their friends.

You begin treating people like million-dollar customers by starting at home, with the members of your family. Remember, they are the most important people in your life. So when you start your day well, first thing in the morning, by making the members of your family feel important and telling them that you love them, you will be more positive, relaxed, and happier for the rest of the day.

Fully 85 percent of your success will be determined by how much people like and respect you, especially in business and sales. Never miss an opportunity to treat people well.

When you practice these seven steps each day for a month, you will see changes and improvements in your life, work, and income that will astonish you. After a month of regular practice, you will have formed a new habit of continuous personal improvement that can carry you onward and upward for the rest of your life.

Be the Best!

Lifelong personal development and the commitment to personal excellence require tremendous dedication, discipline, and willpower. The greatest payoff is that every time you learn and apply something new, your brain releases ***endorphins***, which make you feel happier and more excited about your future.

Every time you learn and apply something new, you will have a greater sense of personal power. Your self-esteem, self-respect, and personal pride will increase. You will feel very much in control of your earning ability, which is one of the most important parts of your life.

In the next chapter, we'll talk about the importance of ***courage***, of overcoming the fears and doubts that hold most people back. It is often the case that we know what we need to do, but we lack the courage to take the risks that accompany trying anything new. Instead, we make excuses for inaction.

Action Exercises:

1. Make a decision today to invest in yourself and getting better, as if your future depends on it—because it does.
2. Identify the most important skills you have that determine the quality and quantity of results you get at your work, and make a plan to get better in each one.
3. If you could wave a magic wand and become absolutely excellent in any one skill, which ***one skill*** would have the greatest impact on your earning ability? Whatever your answer, set that skill as a goal, make a plan, and work on it every day.
4. Set excellent performance in your work as a goal, and then determine exactly what you will need to do every day to join the top 20 percent or better in your field.
5. Look ahead three to five years and determine the new knowledge and skills you will need in order to lead your field in the future. Then start acquiring them today.
6. Select the top person in your field, the one you admire most, and use him or her as a role model for your own development.
7. Commit yourself today to lifelong learning, and never let a day go by without getting better in some area.

Chapter 6

Self-Discipline and Courage

"Courage is not absence of fear;
it is control of fear, mastery of fear."
—MARK TWAIN

You need large amounts of self-discipline to deal courageously with all the fear-inducing events of your life. This is probably why Churchill said, "Courage is rightly considered the foremost of the virtues, for upon it, all others depend."

The fact is that everyone is afraid—and usually of many things. This is normal and natural. Often, fear is necessary to preserve life, prevent injury, and guard against financial mistakes.

So if everyone is afraid, what is the difference between the brave person and the coward? The only difference is that the brave person ***disciplines*** himself to confront, deal with, and act in spite of the fear. In contrast, the coward allows himself to be dominated and controlled by the fear.

Someone once said that—with regard to warfare, although it applies to any situation—"The difference between the hero and the coward is that the hero sticks in there five minutes longer."

Fears Can Be Unlearned

Fortunately, all fears are ***learned***; no one is born with fears. Fears can therefore be unlearned by practicing self-discipline repeatedly with regard to fear until it goes away.

The most common fears that we experience, which often sabotage all hope for success, are the fears of failure, poverty, and loss of money. These fears cause people to avoid risk of any kind and to reject opportunity when it is presented to them. They are so afraid of failure that they are almost paralyzed when it comes to taking any chances at all.

There are many other fears that interfere with our happiness. People fear the loss of love or the loss of their jobs and their financial security. People fear embarrassment or ridicule. People fear rejection and criticism of any kind. People fear the loss of respect or esteem of others. These and many other fears hold us back throughout life.

Fear Paralyzes Action

The most common reaction in a fear situation is the attitude of, "I can't!" This is the fear of failure and loss that stops us from taking action. It is experienced physically, starting in the solar plexus. When people are really afraid, their mouth and throat go dry, their heart starts pounding. Sometimes they breathe shallowly and their stomach churns. Often they feel like getting up and running to the bathroom.

These are all physical manifestations of the ***inhibitive*** negative habit pattern, which we all experience from time to time. Whenever a person is in the grip of fear, he feels like a deer caught in the headlights of a car. This fear paralyzes action. It often shuts down the brain and causes the individual to revert to the "fight-or-flight" reaction. Fear is a terrible emotion that undermines our happiness and can hold us back throughout our lives.

Do the Opposite

Aristotle described courage as the "Golden Mean" between the extremes of cowardice and impetuousness. He taught that "to develop a quality that you lack, act as if you already had that quality in every situation where it is called for." In modern terms, however, we say, "Fake it until you make it."

You can actually change your behavior by affirming, visualizing, and ***acting as if*** you already have the quality you desire. By affirming, by repeating the words, "I can do it!" emphatically whenever you feel afraid for any reason, you can cancel the feeling of "I can't."

Every time you repeat the words "I can do it!" with conviction, you override your fear and increase your confidence. By repeating this affirmation over and over again, you can eventually build your courage and confidence to the point where you are unafraid.

Visualize Yourself as Unafraid

By visualizing yourself performing with confidence and competence in an area where you are fearful, your visual image will eventually be accepted by your subconscious mind as ***instructions*** for your performance. Your self-image, the way you see yourself and think about yourself, is eventually altered by feeding your mind these positive mental pictures of yourself performing at your best.

By using the "act as if" method, you walk, talk, and carry yourself exactly as you would if you were completely ***unafraid*** in a particular situation. You stand up straight, smile, move quickly and confidently, and in every respect act as if you already had the courage that you desire.

The Law of Reversibility says that "if you feel a certain way, you will act in a manner consistent with that feeling." But if you act in a manner consistent with that feeling, even if you don't feel it, the Law of Reversibility will create the feeling that is consistent with your actions.

This is one of the greatest breakthroughs in success psychology. You ***develop*** the courage you desire by disciplining yourself repeatedly to do the thing you fear until that fear eventually disappears—and it will.

Blow Away the Fear

When I work with sales organizations, they often ask me how to help a salesperson break out of a sales slump, especially in a tough economy. I give them a simple formula that is guaranteed to work, every single time. It is called the "100-Call Method." In practicing this method, I instruct the salesperson to go out and call on one hundred prospects as fast as he can, without caring at all whether or not he makes a sale.

When the salesperson doesn't care if he makes a sale, his fear of rejection largely disappears. He stops caring if the prospect he is speaking to is interested or not interested. He has a single focus. It is to make one hundred calls as fast as he possibly can.

One sales organization I work with has a daily prize for the first salesperson who gets rejected ten times each morning. At 8:30 A.M., all the salespeople sit down at their desks and start making calls to try to win the prize. By the time the contest is over, usually by 10 A.M., everyone's fears of rejection have been blown out of their systems. They're ready to call on prospects all day long, not caring at all about the reactions they get.

Learn to Speak on Your Feet

In 1923, Toastmasters International was formed. Its express purpose was to take people who were terrified of public speaking and help them to become confident and competent when speaking on their feet in front of an audience.

According to ***The Book of Lists***, 54 percent of adults rate the fear of public speaking ahead of the fear of death. But Toastmasters International had a solution. They created a system based on what psychologists call "systematic desensitization."

Once a week, at a luncheon or dinner meeting, small groups of Toastmasters come together. Each person is required to stand up and give a short talk on a specified subject in front of a group of his peers. At the end of each talk, the speaker receives applause, positive input, and comments from the other members. At the end of the evening, each person is given a grade on his talk, even if it was only for thirty or sixty seconds.

After six months of attending Toastmaster's meetings, the individual will have stood on his feet and spoken twenty-six times, receiving positive applause and feedback each time. Because of this continuous positive reinforcement, his confidence increases dramatically. As a result of this process, countless Toastmasters have gone on to become excellent public speakers and prominent people in their businesses, organizations, and communities. Their fears of public speaking are gone forever.

Eliminate Two Fears at Once

Psychologists have found that certain fears are bundled together in the subconscious mind, like wires on the same circuit. If you can overcome your fears in one of these areas, you will also eliminate other fears on the same circuit.

The fear of rejection, or call reluctance, seems to be bundled together with the fear of public speaking. When you discipline yourself to join Toastmasters or take a Dale Carnegie course to learn to speak confidently on your feet, your fears of rejection disappear as well. Your level of self-confidence in all your interactions with others increases dramatically. Your whole life changes in a positive way.

Confront Your Fears

Your ability to confront, deal with, and act in spite of your fears is the key to happiness and success. One of the best exercises you can practice is to identify a person or situation in your life of which you are afraid and resolve to deal with that fear situation immediately. Do not allow it to make you unhappy for another minute. Resolve to confront the situation or person and put the fear behind you.

A woman in one of my seminars told me that her boss was a very negative person. He was constantly criticizing and berating her about her work, even though she was one of the highest-rated employees in the organization. He was making her life miserable. She didn't want to give up her job, but she was afraid of confronting him. She asked me what she should do.

I gave her this advice, which I have subsequently given to many other people: The only reason that one person bullies another is he feels he can get away with it. The only way to deal with a bully is to confront him. Bullies are actually cowards at heart, and they will flee from a confrontation.

I told her to do this: The next time your boss criticizes you for any reason, turn to him and say, quite firmly, "I would appreciate if you not talk to me like that ever again. It hurts my feelings and stops me from doing my job the way you want."

I told her to look him straight in the eye after she had finished making this statement. She had tremendous courage. Rather than putting up with this situation any longer, the next time her boss began to berate her, she squared off with him and said those words.

She wrote to me and told me what had happened. Just as I had predicted, he stopped dead in his tracks. He immediately apologized and mumbled and then quickly went back to his office. He never criticized her again. She told me that she could have ended his bad treatment of her many months before if she had only had the courage to confront him directly the first time it happened.

As Eleanor Roosevelt said, "No one can make you feel inferior without your consent."

Move Toward the Fear

When you identify a fear and discipline yourself to move toward it, it grows smaller and more manageable. What's more, as your fears grow smaller, your confidence grows. Soon, your fears lose their control over you.

In contrast, when you back away from a fear-inducing situation or person, your fear grows ***larger*** and ***larger***. Soon it dominates your thinking and feeling, preoccupies you during the day, and often keeps you awake at night.

Leaders Have Two Types of Courage

In leadership, the most common quality is that of ***vision***. Leaders have a clear vision of where they want to take their organizations. Leaders also have a clear vision of where they want to be sometime in the future in their personal lives.

The second most common quality of leaders is that of courage. Leaders have the courage to do whatever is necessary to fulfill their vision. They lead from the front and dare to go forward.

There are two types of courage that you need:

First, you need the courage to ***launch,*** to ***take action***, to take a leap of faith. You need the courage to go "all in" without any guarantee of success and with a high possibility of failure, at least in the short term. The major failing that holds most people back is that in spite of all their best intentions, they don't have the courage to take the first step.

The second type of courage that you need is called "courageous patience." This is the ability to hang in there and continue working and fighting after you have gone all in and before you have yet seen any results or rewards. Many people can muster up the courage to take action toward a new goal, but when they see no immediate result they quickly lose heart and pull back to safety and security. They don't have ***staying power.***

Deal With the Fear Directly

The only way to deal with a fear is to address it head-on. Remind yourself that "denial" is not a river in Egypt. The natural tendency of many people is to deny that they have a problem caused by fear of some kind. They're afraid of confronting it. In turn, it becomes a major source of stress, unhappiness, and psychosomatic illness.

Be willing to deal with the situation or person directly. As Shakespeare said, "Take arms against a sea of troubles, and in so doing, end them."

The companion of fear is ***worry***. Like twin sisters, fear and worry go around together. Mark Twain once wrote,

"I have worried about a lot of things in life, and most of them never happened."

It has been estimated that 99 percent of the things that you worry about never happen. And most of the things that do happen, happen so quickly that you didn't have time to worry about them in the first place.

The Disaster Report

Whenever you are worried about something, fill out a "Disaster Report" on the situation. This will destroy your fear and worry almost instantly. This is often called the "worry buster." The Disaster Report has four parts:

- *First, Define the Worry Situation Clearly.* What exactly are you worried about? Very often, when you take the time to be completely clear about the worry situation, a way to resolve the situation becomes immediately evident.
- ***Second, Identify the Worst Possible Thing That Could Possibly Happen*** if this worry situation were to take place. Would you lose your job? Would you lose your relationship? Would you lose your money? What is the worst thing that could possibly happen? Be clear about this. In many cases, you will see that should the worst occur, it would not ruin you. It might be inconvenient or uncomfortable, but you would eventually recover. You will find that it's probably not worth all the worry that you are devoting to it.
- ***Third, Resolve to Accept the Worst Possible Outcome,*** should it occur. Say to yourself, "Well, if that happens, it won't kill me. I will find a way to get along." Most of the stress of worry comes from denial, from not being willing to face the worst possible thing that could happen. But

once you have resolved to accept the worst (should it occur), all the worry and stress seem to disappear.

- *Fourth, Begin Immediately to Improve on the Worst.* Take every step that you possibly can to make sure that the worst possible outcome does not occur. Take action immediately. Do something. Get on with it. Act quickly. Get so busy making sure that the worst thing does not happen that you have no time to worry.

The Real Antidote

In the final analysis, the only real cure for fear or worry is ***disciplined, purposeful action in the direction of your goals.*** Get so busy working on your goals or the solutions to your problems that you have no time to be afraid or to worry about anything.

When you practice the self-discipline of courage and force yourself to face any fear-inducing situation in your life, your self-esteem goes up, your self-respect increases, and your sense of personal pride grows. You eventually reach the point in life where you are not afraid of *anything.*

Once you have developed the courage to step out in faith, you must then develop the self-discipline of *persistence*, which we will talk about in the next chapter.

Action Exercises:

1. Identify your three biggest fears in life, right now. What are they?

2. Determine what you would do in each of these situations if you were guaranteed of complete success. What actions would you take?
3. What have you always wanted to do but been afraid to attempt? What would you do differently if you were guaranteed success?
4. In what three areas of life and work do you most experience the fears of failure and loss? What steps could you take immediately to confront and eliminate those fears?
5. In what three areas of life do you most experience the fears of criticism, rejection, or embarrassment? How could you confront these fears and overcome them?
6. What one great goal would you set for yourself if you knew you could not fail?
7. What would you do differently in life if you had $20 million in the bank, but only ten years left to live?

Chapter 7

Self-Discipline and Persistence

"Beware of endeavoring to become a great man in a hurry. One such attempt in 10,000 may succeed. These are fearful odds."
—BENJAMIN DISRAELI

Persistence is self-discipline in action. Your ability to persist in the face of all setbacks and temporary failures is essential to success in life.

Napoleon Hill said, "Persistence is to the character of man as carbon is to steel." The primary reason for success is persistence, and, likewise, the primary reason for failure is lack of persistence, quitting too soon.

There is a direct link between self-discipline and self-esteem. Each time you discipline yourself to do what you should do, when you should do it, whether you feel like it or not, your self-esteem increases. This why there is direct relationship between self-esteem and persistence. Each time you persist and force yourself to continue on, even when you feel like quitting, your self-esteem goes up.

Each act of self-discipline strengthens every other act of self-discipline. Every act of persistence strengthens every other act of persistence. When you discipline yourself to persist, over and over, you like and respect yourself more and more. You become stronger and more confident. Eventually, you become ***unstoppable***.

The Reward of Persistence

Persistence is its own reward. Every time you force yourself to persist on a task, whether it is large or small, you feel happier and better about yourself.

When you go the extra mile and do more than you are paid for or more than is expected, your self-esteem goes up. You feel more powerful and in greater control of your life. In your career, when you go the extra mile you put yourself on the side of the angels. The primary difference between winners and losers in life is simple: Winners never quit, and quitters never win.

You can increase your ability to persist by talking to yourself positively. Say these words: "I am unstoppable!" Before you begin any major undertaking, preprogram yourself by telling yourself, "I never give up."

Before you can achieve anything worthwhile in life, you have to pass "the persistence test." This is usually a "snap quiz" sprung on you unexpectedly with no warning. You suddenly face a major setback, problem, temporary failure, or even a complete disaster. When this happens, remind yourself that this is the "testing time." This is when you demonstrate what you are really made of. This is when you show yourself and others the strength of your character and your true determination to succeed.

Your Ability to Respond

Your ability to respond effectively to setbacks—your level of "response-ability"—is the measure of your readiness to succeed. When you experience a major setback or problem, you will feel temporarily stunned. This feeling is very much like a punch in the ***emotional*** solar plexus. You will be stopped for a few seconds or a few minutes. During this period, you will often feel discouraged or experience self-pity. You will say, "Why me?"

However, it is not how far you fall that counts, but rather how high you bounce. Your aim is to bounce back as quickly as possible. Resilience in the face of unexpected reversals is vital to long-term success. Remember the warrior's creed: "I will lay me down to bleed awhile, and then rise and fight again."

Don't be surprised, shocked, or set back when things go wrong. Your best-laid plans will often fall apart. Instead, ***expect*** disappointments and setbacks as a part of life. Take a deep breath, pick up the pieces, and continue onward.

Optimism Gives You Resilience

The most important quality you need for success and persistence is ***optimism***. This is a boundless confidence in yourself and your ability to ultimately succeed. To remain optimistic, you must control and discipline your thinking when things go wrong. Refuse to feel sorry for yourself. Remember, you are not a ***victim***. You are an adult, and you are in charge of your own life. You are doing what you have freely chosen to do. Setbacks come with the territory. They are merely speed bumps on the road to success.

Refuse to blame others or make excuses. When you complain or blame other people, it just makes you feel and sound petty and small, and, what's worse, it takes away your personal power. Whenever you criticize or complain, it makes you feel weaker and reduces your ability to deal effectively with the situation. Instead, greet every setback by repeating, "I am responsible."

Look for the reasons why ***you*** are responsible for what happened rather than trying to pass off the blame onto other people. No excuses.

Be Proactive Versus Reactive

Resolve to focus on the ***solution*** and what can be done ***now***, rather than on what happened and who's to blame. Think in terms of the actions you can take to resolve the situation rather than what went wrong and who is to blame.

To remain optimistic, look for the ***good*** in every situation. When you look for something good, you will always find something good. Furthermore, while you're looking for something good, because your conscious mind can hold only one thought at a time, you will automatically become positive, optimistic, and back in full control.

Seek the ***valuable lesson*** in every problem or difficulty. Every setback you face contains one or more lessons that have been sent to you to help you be more successful in the future. The difference between successes and failures is simple: Failures feel sorry for themselves when things go wrong, whereas successful people look for the valuable lesson they can learn that will help them in the future.

Look for the Gift

Normal Vincent Peale used to say, "When God wants to send you a gift, he wraps it up in a problem. The bigger the gift that God wants to send you, the bigger the problem he wraps it up in."

Instead of concentrating on the problem, look for the ***gift***. Wonderfully enough, you will always find it. What's more, sometimes the gift, or valuable lesson, can be of far greater value than the cost of the problem itself. Sometimes, one lesson that you learn in dealing with a problem can be the key to your long-term success. As Napoleon Hill wrote, "Within every problem or obstacle lays the seed of an equal or greater opportunity or benefit. Your job is to find it."

Continually think of yourself as a strong, powerful, resolute person in the face of adversity. In World War I, a British general was described by his superiors: "There he stands, like an iron peg, driven into the frozen ground, immovable."

Let this be an accurate description of you whenever you face difficulties or problems of any kind. Resolve to stand like an iron peg driven into the frozen ground.

Resolve in Advance

When you resolve in advance that you will never give up, your success is virtually guaranteed. In the final analysis, nothing can really stop you but ***yourself.***

In life, it doesn't matter how many times you get knocked down. All that matters is how many times you get back up. If you continue to get back up and press onward, you must eventually reach your goal.

Each time you exert your self-discipline to persist in the face of adversity, you also increase your self-esteem and self-confidence. Then, as your self-esteem increases, you feel stronger, more powerful, and more unstoppable. When you feel better and stronger, you become more capable of persisting the next time—and then the time after that.

By disciplining yourself to persist in the face of all adversity, you put your life onto an upward spiral of self-esteem, self-discipline, and persistence until you eventually become like a force of nature.

Persistence is self-discipline in action.

In Part Two, you will learn the specific things you can do to apply these principles to the practical areas of life, to achieve greater success in your work and career, and to fulfill your potential in the months and years ahead.

Action Exercises:

1. Identify one area in your life in which you need to persist even harder to achieve your goal, and then take action in that area.

2. Identify a goal in your life that you did not accomplish because you failed to persist through to completion. What steps could you take today to succeed in that area?
3. Identify one big goal that you achieved because you persisted and refused to give up, no matter how difficult it became.
4. Decide on your major definite purpose in life, the one goal that, if you achieved it, would have the greatest positive impact on your life.
5. Write down your goal clearly, make a detailed plan of action to accomplish it, and then tell yourself that "failure is not an option."
6. Make a decision today that you will persist until you succeed, no matter what happens, because "I am unstoppable."
7. Resolve to set and achieve one important goal, overcoming the inevitable difficulties, problems and setbacks you will experience, and to work at it until you succeed. Repeat this process over and over until persistence becomes a habit.

PART II

Self-Discipline in Business, Sales, and Finances

In this part, you will learn how to develop the discipline necessary to join the top 10 percent of people in your field. You will learn how to increase your productivity, performance, output, and results. You will learn how to become one of the most respected and esteemed people in your organization and your industry.

Chapter 8

Self-Discipline and Work

"Leaders aren't born; they are made. And they are made just like anything else, through hard work. And that's the price we'll have to pay to achieve that goal, or any goal."
—VINCE LOMBARDI

There is perhaps no area of your life where self-discipline has a greater impact on your future than in your work. Yet, if you're like most people, from the time you start in the morning and then continuing throughout the day, you are surrounded by people and events that draw you away from doing the things that are most important. However, it is through doing your most important tasks that you move onward and upward, quickly and dependably in your career.

A group of senior executives was asked, "What are the most important qualities that a person would need to be promoted in your company?" Of these executives, 85 percent agreed that the most important qualities are

1. The ability to set priorities and work on high-value tasks; and
2. The discipline to get the job done quickly and well.

It seems that these two qualities are more helpful for career success than anything else a person can do. Diligent, disciplined, focused work will enable you to consistently and predictably get more done, get paid more, and get promoted faster throughout your career than the average person.

Separate the Relevant from the Irrelevant

I've mentioned the Pareto Principle—the 80/20 rule—several times in this book, and it applies again here. Fully 80 percent of the value of what you accomplish will come from 20 percent of the things you do. Your job, then, is to identify those top 20 percent of your tasks and then concentrate single-mindedly on doing them quickly and well.

Chapter 13 discusses time management in detail, but for now, let's take a look at the flip side of good time management—***poor*** time management. According to Robert Half International, the average employee ***wastes*** about 50 percent of his or her time on nonwork-related activities:

- Thirty-seven percent of work time is wasted on idle conversation on personal subjects with coworkers, conversations that have nothing whatsoever to do with the job at hand.

- The other 13 percent of wasted time is consumed by coming in late or leaving early, by long lunches and coffee breaks, by surfing the Internet, reading the newspaper, or conducting personal business during the day.

Even worse, when people who waste a lot of time actually settle down and get to work, they spend too much time on low-value tasks and activities. As a result, they get very little done, which then causes them to feel that they are under continual pressure to get caught up.

Unfortunately, when you waste time at work, your work does not go away. It continually builds, like an avalanche overhang. Deadlines come closer and closer. Stress mounts up until you finally force yourself to do the job, usually at the last minute, and then you often make expensive mistakes.

Develop an Excellent Reputation

There is nothing that will bring you more quickly to the attention of people who can help you than for you to develop a reputation for hard, disciplined work, every hour of every day.

Average employees increase their income at only about 3 percent per year, which is just about the rate of inflation or cost-of-living increases. In other words, if you're an average employee, you're not really making any more money from year to year. Rather, you're just keeping up with your expenses. But the top 20 percent in most fields increase their income anywhere from 10 to 25 percent per year—which is also compounded, year after year.

The top 20 percent of people at work earn 80 percent of the money. The bottom 80 percent of employees have no choice but to share the 20 percent of the money that is left over. They must scramble for the crumbs that fall off the tables of the highly productive people in their fields.

You Can Double Your Income!

When I say to people in my seminars that you should set a goal to "double your income" in the months and years ahead, people react in different ways. Often, at the break, someone will come up to me and say, "You don't understand my company. There is no way that I could double my income at my current company. They simply would not pay me that amount of money."

Having heard this before, I then ask them the critical question: "Is there ***anyone*** at your company who earns twice as much as you?"

The person who I am talking to will always agree that, "Yes, there are people in my company who earn two or three times as much as I do."

I then make the key point, "So your company is quite willing to pay ***some*** people twice as much as they pay you. They're just not willing to pay ***you*** twice as much. Why is that?"

Then suddenly the light goes on. This individual realizes that it is not ***the company*** that is not willing to pay the money. It is ***the individual*** who is not contributing enough to be worth that additional money. The responsibility is ***his,*** not the company's.

The Law of Three Helps You Prioritize

When we coach entrepreneurs, executives, and business owners, we take them through an exercise that is designed to help them double their productivity, performance, and output within twelve months—sometimes, even, within thirty days. It's simple. Here's how it works.

First, make a list of all the things that you do in a week or a month, from the time you start work on Monday morning through to the end of the week. Write everything down, both small and large, including checking your e-mail and returning phone calls.

Then, review this list and ask this key question:

> "If I could do only *one* thing on this list, all day long, which one task or activity contributes the most value to my company?"

As you go over your list, the correct answer will probably jump out at you. Whatever it is, put a circle around it.

Then ask the second question:

> "If I could do only *two* things on this list, all day long, which would be the second task or activity?"

Review your list again, and identify your second most important task in terms of contribution to your company.

Finally, ask the question once more:

> "If I could do only *three* things on this list, all day long, what would be the third item?"

We call this the "Law of Three." The Law of Three says that there are three primary things you do that contribute 90 percent or more of your value to your company or organization. Your job is to identify those three critical tasks and then ***discipline yourself*** to do them ***all day long.*** All of your other minor tasks will be support tasks, complementary tasks, enjoyable tasks, or useless tasks. They will be little things that you have often gotten into the habit of doing as a way of unconsciously avoiding the big, difficult, important tasks that can make a tremendous difference in your work and career.

Calculate Your Hourly Rate

Another way for you to double your income is for you to use the "hourly rate" method of calculating your personal value and your time allocation. First, determine the amount that you earn each hour. You do this by dividing your annual income by the number 2,000 (which is the roughly the number of hours that an entrepreneur or executive works each year in our society: 40 hours a week × 50 weeks a year).

For example, if you earn $50,000 a year, divided by 2,000, your hourly rate would be $25. If you earn $100,000 per year, divided by 2,000, your hourly rate would be $50.

Whatever it is, from that moment onward, resolve to do ***only*** those things that pay you your hourly rate or better. Refuse to do those things that someone else can do at a lower hourly rate than you. Do not waste your time doing things of low value or no value while your other important tasks are building up.

• • •

Get on the Same Page About What Work Is Most Important

Once you have made a list of all the results you feel you have been hired to accomplish and you have determined the three most important things you do to justify your hourly rate, take your list of key activities to your boss and have your boss organize your job based on his or her priorities. You need to do this because you must be sure.

Benjamin Tregoe, cofounder of the Kepner-Tregoe consulting firm and author of ***The Rational Manager***, once said, "The very worst use of time is to do very well what need not be done at all."

Yet it is amazing how many people are working hard on tasks that are of little or no value to their bosses. No matter how well you do an ***unimportant*** task, it does not help you. Even worse, working on low-value tasks keeps you from working on the most important things you could be doing. Hard work on the wrong job can actually ***sabotage*** your career.

The happiest days you will have at work will be when you are working on those tasks that your boss considers to be most important. The unhappiest days at work will be when you and your boss are at cross-purposes and not getting along primarily because you are not completing the jobs that are most important to him and to his career.

Your goal is to be paid more and promoted faster. Your goal is to become one of the most valuable and highest paid people in your field. Your job is first, to make yourself valuable, and then to make yourself ***indispensable*** to your company. This requires first and foremost that you are always working on those tasks your boss considers most important.

Work All the Time You Work

The key to doubling your productivity and output—and eventually your income—is to really ***work*** all the time you are at work. Simply put, when you work, ***work***. Don't waste time. Don't delay. Don't chat with coworkers or sit around drinking coffee. Don't read the newspaper or surf the Internet. When you come into work in the morning, put your head down, and then work all day long.

The biggest time wasters in the world of work are other people who want to talk with you, distract you, delay you, and take up the time that you should be spending on high-value tasks. When a time waster approaches you and says, "Do you have a minute to talk?" you reply by saying, "Yes, but not now. Why don't we talk at lunchtime, or after work? In the meantime, I have to get this job finished. I have to get ***back to work***."

When you tell people that you are under the gun, that you have to get a task finished for your boss, they will usually leave you alone. If you do this often enough, they will develop the habit of leaving you alone and, instead, find someone else with whom to waste time.

Keep yourself motivated and focused by talking to yourself in a positive way. Your mantra from now on should be, "Back to work! Back to work! Back to work!"

Whenever you find yourself slowing down on a major task, begin repeating to yourself those magic words, “Back to work!”

Who Works Hardest? The Secret Survey

Imagine that an outside company is going to do a study of all the people who work in your organization. They are going to give each person a list of all the employees and ask him to rate his fellow employees in terms of who works the hardest, the second hardest, and so on.

They are then going to give this list of people, organized from the hardest worker down to the laziest, to your superiors. This list is going to be used to determine who gets paid more and promoted faster than others.

Now, imagine that this survey is already being taken, but in secret. The fact is, in any organization, everyone knows who works harder than anyone else. Everyone knows who works less and who does not pull his weight. ***Everyone knows***—it’s not a secret at all.

Resolve today that, if a survey like this were to be taken, one year from today, you would “win” the contest. Resolve today that you are going to develop the reputation for being the hardest-working person in your business. This will do more to help you than almost anything else.

When you are surrounded by time-wasting people and situations, it takes tremendous self-discipline to work all the time you are at work. You must constantly fight against distractions and interruptions so you can get back to work.

The Success Formula

When I began my career working for a large company, I was the low man on the totem pole. Everyone had been there longer than me and was ahead of me in the company pecking order. Even though I was in my early thirties, I still had no idea how to play the game or what to do to get ahead in the cutthroat, corporate competition that existed.

Somewhat by accident, I stumbled onto the formula that made me successful. It was simple. Whenever my boss gave me something to do, I did it immediately. Like a dog chasing after a thrown stick, I would immediately throw myself at the task, complete it, and hurry back to my boss with the finished job.

Initially, he would smile and say something like, "I didn't really need it that quickly, but thank you for getting it done."

Ask for More Responsibility

When I was caught up with my work, instead of relaxing, I would go to my boss and say, "I'm all caught up. I want more work to do. I want more responsibility." These words became my mantra: "I want more responsibility."

Again my boss, who was preoccupied with an enormous number of projects, would say something like, "Okay, leave it with me; I'll think about what else I can give you to do."

Every day, like a broken record, I would go to my boss at the end of the day and say, "I'm all caught up; I would like more responsibility."

Bit by bit, he began to toss me "sticks." He would give me a little task to do to keep me busy. Whatever it was, I would go out immediately, complete the task, and bring him the results. I would then say, "I'm all caught up. I want more responsibility."

Within six months, he began to see me as the "go-to guy." Whenever he had something he needed done quickly, he passed by everyone else and gave it to me. He knew that whatever he asked me to do, I would do it quickly.

Time Is of the Essence

Once, my boss asked me to fly to Reno to begin development work on a property that the company was purchasing. He told me I could go sometime in the next couple of weeks. Instead, I left the next morning. I went straight to the lawyer who was handling the transaction and then to the engineer who was in charge of the development work. I immediately sensed that something was seriously wrong with this land purchase. I didn't know what it was, but I went from person to person, asking questions and gathering information.

By the end of the day, just a few hours before this $2 million transaction was set to close and the money would change hands forever, I found that we were about to be sold a piece of land that had no water and was therefore ***undevelopable***. Because of complex laws and limited riparian rights (i.e., water rights), the property was a worthless piece of ground that could not be developed within the next hundred years. If we had proceeded with the purchase, we would have lost $2 million!

I immediately stopped the transaction, demanded that the lawyer cut me a certified check for the $250,000 deposit that was in his trust account, and flew home to my boss to tell him the story. As you can imagine, my boss was very happy with what I had done.

The Big Payoff

From that day forward, I received more and more responsibilities. Within another year, I was running three divisions of the company and had a staff of forty-two people in three cities. I later learned that my boss paid me more money than anyone else who had ever worked for him, and he did so all on the basis of results and profitability.

This is why whenever people ask me how to succeed in business by ***really*** trying, I give them the same advice: Whatever your boss gives you to do, do it quickly and well. Then, go and ask for more responsibility. And when you get it, do the job quickly and well until you get a reputation for being the person who does things fast. This will help you advance in your career more than any other reputation you could develop.

Pay the Price

Here is a simple three-part formula for success at work: Come in a little ***earlier***, work a little ***harder***, and stay a little ***later***. This will move you so far ahead of your competitors that they will never catch up.

Come into work one hour earlier, before anyone else arrives. Use that time to plan and organize your day and get started on your most important tasks. Make sure that whatever time your boss comes to work, you are always there working before he arrives.

Second, work a little harder. Don't waste time. Don't chat with coworkers. Work through lunchtime so that you can get on top—and stay on top—of your main tasks and responsibilities.

Third, work one hour later than your coworkers. If they leave at five o'clock, you leave at six. Use that extra time to complete your important tasks and get yourself organized for the following day.

When you come in one hour earlier, work through lunch, and work one hour later, you add ***three*** full productive hours to your day. Because there are no interruptions when you work during these time periods, you will actually accomplish two or three times as much as you would during your other work hours, when you are constantly interrupted by other people and telephone calls.

In fact, you can double or even triple your productivity, performance, and output by simply adding these three hours to your workday. The best news is that by coming in earlier and leaving later, you don't lose anything. You merely avoid the traffic tie-ups and slow-downs that most people suffer through on their ways to and from work.

The Forty Plus Formula

To succeed faster at work, use the "Forty Plus Formula." This formula says that you can tell where you are going to be five years from now by looking at the number of hours that you put in today ***in excess of*** forty hours each week.

If all you do is put in the regular forty hours that everyone else puts in, all you will do is survive. Your annual increases will be 3 or 4 percent. You will have a "job," but your income increases will go up at the same rate as everyone else.

It is when you put in ***more than forty hours*** that you give yourself an advantage over most of the other people in your company—and your business. Make it a ***habit*** to do more than what you are paid for. Discipline yourself to put in more than you take out. Every hour that you work over forty hours a week is an investment in your future success.

The highest paid people in America, in every field, work fifty to sixty hours per week. The average self-made millionaire works fifty-nine hours per week. This is equal to five twelve-hour days or six ten-hour days. Most successful people, at the beginning of their careers, worked six days a week—sometimes seven. Moreover, they ***worked*** all the time they were at work. They didn't waste time. They realized that in order to reap a great harvest later in their career, they had to sow a lot of seeds in the springtime of their career.

Look the Part: Dress for Success

Finally, you need to discipline yourself to look the part. Remember, "birds of a feather flock together." When it comes to presentation, this means that people like to promote others who look like them. Your bosses are very sensitive to the appearance of their staff. They like to promote people who they are proud to introduce to their friends and colleagues. Be sure that you dress and groom in such a way that your boss would be proud to take you out for lunch and introduce you to others as a representative of his or her company.

Each morning before you go to work, look in the mirror and ask yourself, "Do I look like one of the top people in my field?" If you don't, go back and change—and keep changing until you look like one of the top people in your business.

Learn how to ***dress for success***. Read books and articles, or ask others for advice. Look at the most successful people in your business and dress the way they do. Dress for the job ***two*** levels above your current job. Remember that fully 95 percent of the first impression you make on other people will be determined by your dress and grooming. Make sure that first impression—and then the second and third impressions—are consistent with the message you want to send.

Many people work their entire lives without realizing that by putting forward a little extra effort, working a little harder, and focusing on higher-value tasks, they could become one of the most valuable people in their organizations. When you discipline yourself to continually increase the value of your contribution to your company, you will put your career on the fast track and virtually guarantee yourself a wonderful future.

In the next chapter, you will learn that your work behaviors naturally determine your ascension to leadership, and you will see how self-discipline is essential to fulfilling your potential as a leader.

Action Exercises:

1. Make a decision today that you are going to become one of the top 20 percent of people in your company—and your industry. What should you or could you do differently?
2. Make a list of everything you do in your job and then identify the three tasks that contribute the greatest value to your work and company.
3. Set a new work schedule for yourself and begin to start earlier, work harder, and stay later until it becomes a habit.

4. Identify the most important results you are expected to achieve in your job, and then work on those results all day long.
5. Determine the person who is the best dressed and groomed in your company, and then resolve to use him/her as a role model for your own appearance.
6. Decide today that, from now on, you are going to actually work all the time you are at work and that you are going to develop the reputation for being the hardest working person in your company.
7. Develop a sense of urgency. Resolve to move fast when you are given a job or opportunity. This can change your life.

Chapter 9

Self-Discipline and Leadership

"Nothing is more harmful to the service than the neglect of discipline; for it is discipline more than numbers that gives one army superiority over another."
—GEORGE WASHINGTON

Leadership and self-discipline go hand in hand. It is not possible to imagine an effective leader who lacks self-discipline, willpower, self-control, and self-mastery. The overarching characteristic of a leader is that he is in complete control of himself and of every situation.

There has seldom been a time in history when leaders were so needed and so much in demand as today. We need leaders at every level of society, both in the profit and nonprofit sectors. We need leaders in our families, businesses, places of worship, community organizations, and, especially, politics. We need men and women who take their responsibilities seriously and are willing to step forward to take command of the situation.

Fortunately, leadership is ***learnable.*** Leaders are developed—usually self-developed—over time through hard work, experience, and training. As Peter Drucker once said, "There may be natural-born leaders, but there are so few of them, that they make no difference in the great scheme of things."

Four Stages of Development

In your career in business, you progress through four levels of activity and attainment. First, you start off as an ***employee,*** with limited knowledge and experience. Then, as you grow, learn, and develop the ability to get results, you evolve upward and become a ***supervisor,*** with responsibility for the performance and results of other people.

As you continue to move up the scale of supervision, improving your ability to get things done through others from directly overseeing the work of employees, you become a ***manager***, someone who assigns work to people with demonstrated competence in certain areas. Managers have a larger view, and this comes with greater responsibilities.

As you move up the scale of management, becoming more knowledgeable and effective and getting more and better results from more and different people, you reach the highest level, that of a ***leader.*** At this stage, you are responsible for determining ***what*** is to be done rather than ***how*** it is to be done.

It is said that "some leaders are made, some are born, and some people have leadership thrust upon them."

Leaders emerge or are promoted to deal with a situation requiring leadership ability. In its simplest terms, the role of the leader is to "take responsibility for results."

The primary reason that people are promoted into increasingly higher levels of leadership is that they demonstrate the ability to get the required results at each level. The ongoing question of the leader is always, "What results are expected of me?" Clarity is essential.

The main reason that some people are not promoted into greater leadership position—or perhaps they are even fired—is because of "failure to execute." They do not do the most important jobs expected of them, nor do they get the results demanded of them.

Leaders Have Vision

The first quality of leadership, based on 3,300 studies of leaders done by James MacPherson, is the quality of ***vision***. Leaders have vision. They have the ability to project forward into the future and develop a clear picture of where they want their organizations to go. They then have the ability to share this vision with others and gain others' commitment to make this vision a reality.

You become a leader when you accept responsibility for results. You become a leader when you begin to think, act, and talk like a leader. You become a leader when you develop a ***vision*** for yourself and for your company, your life, or your area of responsibility.

There are hundreds of books written about leadership and the importance of vision. Yet they can be boiled down to a single principle. A military leader has a vision of ***victory***, from which he never deviates. A business leader has a vision of ***success*** for the business based on excellent performance, to which he or she is completely committed.

A Leader Is a Standard Bearer

The leader sets the standard for the organization. It is not possible for anyone in the organization to have a clearer vision or to aspire to a higher standard of excellence than the leader. For this reason, the leader is the role model, the one who sets the tone and the morale for everyone in the organization. The personality and influence of the leader affect everyone below him in the company, organization, or department.

You cannot ***raise*** morale in a business; it filters down from the top, from the leader. The behavior of the leader influences and affects the behavior of everyone else. If the leader is positive, confident, and upbeat, everyone in the organization will be influenced by this behavior and will be more positive, confident, and upbeat as well.

Walk the Talk

When you become a leader, you must discipline yourself to be "leaderlike." You must walk, talk, and act the part of a leader. You become a different person with different responsibilities.

When you are working your way up, you are a part of the staff or the sales team. When you become a manager, you are part of management. This means that when you are part of the staff, your orientation is upward and sideways, but when you become a leader, your orientation is downward, toward all the people for whom you are responsible.

Perhaps the most important behavior of a leader is for you to discipline yourself to be a ***role model.*** Imagine that everyone is watching you and patterning everything they do and say based on your behavior.

When you become a leader you no longer have the luxury to "let it all hang out." From the time you are promoted into leadership, you have a special responsibility to discipline and control your words and behaviors in such a way so that you bring about the best possible results for your organization and for other people.

Set the Standards

The leader sets the standards for the organization's behavior, quality of work, personal organization, time management, and appearance. In excellent organizations, the leader is the person who everyone looks up to and wants to emulate.

In most cases, the leader works harder than others in the company. The leader appears to be more committed, determined, courageous, visionary, and persistent than anyone else. The leader sets a tone that everyone wants to emulate.

The leader also sets the standard for how people are treated in the organization. When the leader treats people with courtesy, consideration, and concern, it quickly becomes known that these are the standards to which others must adhere.

Set Values and Principles

In addition to a clear vision for the organization, the leader must have a set of values and organizing principles that guide behavior and decision making. Everyone must know what the leader and the company stand for and believe in. The job of the leader, then, is to articulate this vision of excellent performance within the constraints of high ethical standards at all times. He or she must walk the talk and live the values and behaviors he or she teaches.

The very best standard for a leader is the Golden Rule: "Do unto others as you would have them do unto you."

> For example, when Jack Welch was the president of General Electric, he encouraged managers to treat each employee as if that employee might be promoted over his head sometime in the future and he might find himself working under the person who is now working below him. This way of thinking ensured that managers treated their staff with a high degree of respect and courtesy.

Seven Principles of Leadership

To be an effective leader, there are seven principles you must incorporate into your leadership behavior and activities.

1. *Clarity:* This is perhaps your most important responsibility. You must be absolutely clear about who you are and what you stand for. You must be absolutely clear about your vision and where you want to lead your people. You must be absolutely clear about the goals and objectives of the organization and how they are to be obtained.

   Especially, you must be absolutely clear about the values, mission, and purpose of the organization and what it stands for. Everyone around you and below you must know exactly why they are doing what they do and what their company has been formed to accomplish.
2. *Competence:* As the leader, you must set a standard of excellent performance for the organization as well as for every person and function in the company. Your goal must be for your company to be as good as, or better than, your very best competitor. You must be continually seeking ways to improve the quality of your products and services to your customers.
3. *Commitment*: The leader is absolutely committed to the success of the organization and believes completely that this organization is the best in the business or will be the best in the future. This passionate commitment to the organization—and to success and achievement—motivates and inspires people to do their best work and put their whole hearts into their jobs.

4. *Constraints:* The job of the leader is to identify the constraints or limiting factors that set the speed at which the company achieves its most important goals of revenue and profitability. The leader then allocates people and resources to alleviate those constraints and remove the obstacles so it can perform as one of the best in the industry.
5. *Creativity*: The leader is open to new ideas of all kinds and from all sources. The leader is continually encouraging people to find faster, better, cheaper, and easier ways to produce excellent products and services and to take better care of customers.
6. ***Continuous Learning:*** The leader is personally committed to reading, listening, and upgrading his or her personal knowledge and skills as an executive. The leader should attend additional seminars and courses to improve his or her skills and abilities.

   At the same time, the leader encourages everyone in the organization to learn and grow as a normal and natural part of business life. The leader provides time and resources for training and development. The leader knows that the best companies have the best-trained people. The second-best companies have the second-best trained people. And the third-best companies have the least-trained people—and are on their way out of business.
7. ***Consistency:*** The leader has the self-discipline to be consistent, dependable, reliable, calm, and predictable in all situations. One of the great com-

forts of business life is for an employee to know that the leader is completely consistent and reliable. An effective leader does not change from day to day. The leader is not "blown in the wind" by each new situation, problem, or emergency that arises. Instead, the leader is calm, positive, and confident—especially under pressure.

The Inevitable Crisis

The only thing that is inevitable in the life of the leader is the ***crisis***. When you rise to a position of leadership, you will experience crises repeatedly—crises that are unpredictable, unbidden, and often capable of seriously damaging the organization.

It is in the crisis that the leader demonstrates his competence. In times of crisis, the leader becomes calm, cool, objective, and completely in control. The leader asks questions and gathers information. The leader assesses the situation accurately and makes whatever decisions are necessary to minimize the damage or cut the losses.

Great leaders discipline themselves to keep their fears and misgivings ***private***. They do not share their concerns with their staffs, knowing that this can cause confusion and loss of morale. Instead, the leader asks a lot of questions, probes deeply into situations so that he or she understands them thoroughly, and keeps his or her feelings private.

As far as the members of the organization are concerned, the leader is always calm, positive, relaxed, and in complete control—no matter what is happening.

Self-Control and Leadership

There is a direct relationship between your ability to discipline yourself and your behaviors and your readiness to lead. It is only when you prove to others that you are in complete control of yourself that they develop the confidence to put you in a leadership position—and keep you there.

The leader realizes that everything he says to or about another person is magnified. The leader therefore praises and encourages people, both in their presence and when they are not around. He never says anything negative that could be misinterpreted or that could demotivate or offend another person. If he has problems with someone, he addresses him privately, out of sight and earshot of anyone else.

Leadership Qualities

Leaders discipline themselves to plan, prepare, organize, and check every detail. They take nothing for granted. They ask questions to ensure that they have a complete understanding of a situation, problem, or difficulty.

Great leaders act as if they own the entire company. They accept a high level of personal responsibility. The leader never complains, makes excuses, or blames others for problems.

Leaders are intensely ***action-oriented***. They gather information carefully and make the decisions that are necessary.

They set measures and standards and hold others to them. They insist that the job be done quickly and well.

Leaders Rise to the Top

Leaders rise to the top of an organization, as cream rises in milk. When you accept complete responsibility for getting results, concentrate single-mindedly on completing your most important tasks, continually upgrade your knowledge and skills as well as your ability to contribute value to your company, and treat other people with kindness and consideration, you will emerge as a natural leader.

As you demonstrate your ability to make an increasingly valuable contribution to your organization, people above, below, and on both sides of you will want you to be promoted into leadership and will support you when you reach that position. One of your primary aims in life is to walk, talk, act, speak, and treat others as a leader would. Eventually, your position will be equal to your performance.

In the next chapter, you will learn how to develop and practice the disciplines necessary to be more successful in your business life and activities.

Action Exercises:

1. Ask yourself, "What results are expected of me?" and then concentrate single-mindedly on getting those results every day.

2. See yourself as the leader of your organization and ask yourself, "What kind of a company would this company be if everyone in it were just like me?"
3. Create a clear, exciting vision for yourself and your organization based on success and excellent performance.
4. Identify the most important people in your business world and determine how you will have to behave toward them to get them to perform at their best.
5. Resolve in advance that, when the inevitable crisis occurs, you will respond in a calm, controlled, and intelligent manner.
6. Clarify the exact values and principles you believe in and stand for, and then share them with the people around you.
7. Treat each person around you as if he is competent, valuable, and important. This is the key to gaining the loyalty and commitment that you require as a leader.

Chapter 10

Self-Discipline and Business

"The quality of self denial in the pursuit of a longer term goal, and indeed, the willpower to maintain that level of self denial, is an excellent training for the boardroom."

—John Viney

Most people will work in or for a business or own a business in the course of their lifetimes. The achievement of business success demands high levels of discipline from you in every area of business activity, both large or small. Without self-discipline and self-control in business, no success is possible.

There is no area of activity that demands more self-discipline than starting and operating a successful business in our current economy.

The first law of economics is ***scarcity***. As a rule, there is never enough of anything for everyone who wants it. Specifically, there are never enough customers for you to sell everything you want to sell. There are never enough sales revenues to help you achieve all your financial goals. There are never sufficient profits to enable you to expand as much as you want. Especially, there are never enough good people to work with and for you to help you achieve your business goals.

The Law of Competition

If the first law of economics is scarcity, then the first law of business is ***competition***. It requires tremendous focus and discipline to do the things necessary to attract the scarce money of customers toward purchasing ***your*** product or service.

To not only survive but also thrive, you must compete continually against all other uses of the same amount of money that you want to charge for what you sell.

The first discipline of business success is that you offer a product or service that people want, need, and will pay for at a price they will accept—a price that is competitive with every other business that wants the same customer dollar.

You must be completely honest with your product/service mix to ensure that it is well suited to the current market. This is an area where false assumptions or incorrect conclusions can lead to business failure. This answer is continually changing as competition and customer tastes also change.

The Customer Is Always Right

Every week, I speak to business people who are unhappy with their level of sales and profitability. They insist that their product or service is excellent and that people should be buying from them in much larger quantities. In each case, I have to gently point out to them that the only proof that their product or service is truly attractive or valuable is that people buy it willingly—and then buy it again and tell their friends to buy it as well.

According to the experts, fully 70 percent of your business decisions will turn out to be wrong in the fullness of time. This is the ***average***. When you are a new businessperson or starting a new business, you will be wrong even more often than this. It is not unusual for an entrepreneur to be wrong 90 percent of the time in the beginning of his career.

It requires tremendous self-discipline and character to face the possibility that you could be wrong in your most cherished assumptions and beliefs. Nonetheless, this discipline is essential if you are going to minimize your mistakes, cut your losses, and redirect your resources toward offering customers more of the things that they really want, need, and are willing to pay for today.

All business investment and business start-ups require a high level of optimism. You must believe in the future possibilities of your business along with your new products and services. You must have so much confidence in their marketability that you are willing to undertake financial risk and invest many hours, weeks, and even years to achieve your business goals, and you must do all this with no real guarantee of success.

At the same time, you need discipline to curb your confidence, to remain objective and realistic. Overconfidence in business can lead to business mistakes, financial losses, and even bankruptcy.

You Must Be Better

Because of the aggressive and determined nature of your competition, in order to simply survive, you must discipline yourself to be equal to or better than your competitors. After all, your competitors get out of bed every morning thinking about how they can put ***you*** out of business. They want to take away your customers and your sales. They want to get your profits. They want as much of your business as they can possibly get. To increase your probabilities of success against such competition, you must make every effort to out-think them.

When you start a business or a new venture within a business, you require the discipline to do your homework thoroughly, in advance. You create a complete business plan before you start operations, and you continue to update it and revise it every year thereafter. The discipline of advanced planning can spell the difference between success and failure.

Challenge Your Assumptions

Most business ideas do not work, at least in their original form. As Peter Drucker said, "Errant assumptions lie at the root of every failure." A major reason for business failure is that business owners or executives rely on assumptions that are not tested. They assume that the product or service is excellent in comparison with others. They assume that they can sell a sufficient number of those products or services—and do so at a profit. They further assume that those profits will be substantial enough to make this investment of time and money more attractive than any other use of the same amount of time or funds. All of these assumptions must be tested carefully before any irrevocable commitment is made.

According to the Kaufman Foundation on Entrepreneurship, 95 percent of entrepreneurs and small business owners in America earn less than $50,000 per year. Why is this? It is not because they lack the energy, intelligence, or ability to earn more. The very fact that a person has the courage and resourcefulness to start a new business means that he or she has above-average levels of natural talent.

The reason why so many entrepreneurs underachieve and fail is that they lack discipline. They lack the discipline to carefully study every aspect of the business before committing to it. They lack the discipline to test their assumptions rather than jumping to conclusions and hoping for the best. ***Don't let this happen to you.***

Identify Your Ideal Customer

You need discipline to identify and determine your ideal customer: the exact person who can and will buy your product or service in sufficient quantities and at the price you need to charge in order to justify going into this area of business in the first place.

You need the discipline—based on trial, error, and persistence—to develop a marketing plan that generates a steady and predictable stream of new leads for your business. To market effectively, you must be clear about your ***competitive advantage*** and your ***unique selling proposition***: What is it about your product or service that makes it superior and more valuable for a customer than any other similar product or service being offered today?

You need the discipline to develop a complete sales system, from beginning to end, that converts qualified leads into solid customers. It is amazing how many businesses just assume that the product or service will sell itself—whether they have a superior sales system or not!

Know Your True Costs

You need the discipline to determine accurate costs and the proper pricing of your products and services. Wal-Mart has become the biggest retailer in history largely because of its expertise in this area. It's amazing how many businesses are selling products and services at a loss because they have never accurately totaled all the costs of bringing that product or service to market in the first place. You've heard the old saying, "We lose money on every item we sell, but we try to make it up on the volume." Obviously, that's not possible!

You need a quality control system in order to ensure that every product or service that you sell is of such high quality that your customers are so satisfied that they happily buy from you again—and tell their friends.

You need the discipline to develop a customer service policy, one in which you treat your customers so well that they become loyal to you and choose you over any of your competitors.

The Purpose of a Business Is to Please Its Customers

What is the purpose of a business? The purpose of a business is to ***create and keep a customer*** in a cost-effective manner. Profits are ***not*** the purpose of a business. Profits are the result of ***creating and keeping a sufficient number of customers*** who yield a sufficient number of profits after all costs.

What is the key measure of business success? The answer is ***customer satisfaction***. Every effort and activity of your business must be aimed at satisfying customers in a manner that is better than any other competitor.

What is the measure of customer satisfaction? The answer is ***repeat business.*** It is only when customers buy from you ***again*** that you demonstrate that you have fulfilled the promise you made to them when you got them to purchase the first time. A resale to a satisfied customer requires one tenth of the time and expense as a sale to a brand new customer. All successful businesses rely on repeat business, which is possible only with high levels of customer satisfaction. This is a real discipline.

What is the key to long-term profitability? The answer is ***recommendations and referrals.***

The ultimate question that determines the long-term success or failure of your business is, "Based on your experience with us, would you recommend us to others?"

You can survive and thrive only when the majority of your customers are so happy with your products and services that they will encourage their friends and associates to buy from you as well. Since a referral from a satisfied customer is fifteen times easier to sell to than a cold call (which means it costs only one fifteenth as much), referral business is the key to your future. You require tremendous focus and discipline to develop and maintain customer service policies that cause people to buy from you, then buy again, and then recommend you to their friends.

Set High Standards

You require the discipline to set standards of excellent performance in every area of your business and then to continually strive to get even better. You need to practice the CANEI Formula, which stands for, "Continuous and Never-Ending Improvement." No matter how high your level of quality is today, you can never be satisfied. You must continually be raising the bar on yourself—and on everyone within your area of responsibility.

You require the self-discipline to work long, hard hours for many months and even years to get to the top in your business. The average entrepreneur, business owner, or self-made millionaire in American works fifty-nine hours per week. Some entrepreneurs even work seventy to eighty hours per week in the first few years of building their businesses. You must be prepared to discipline yourself to put in this amount of time and level of hard work if you want to be the best and get to the top of your field.

Think About the Solution

To succeed in business, you need the self-discipline to be ***proactive*** rather than ***reactive***. You need to focus on ***solutions*** rather than problems. You need to concentrate on the most important thing you could possibly be doing every hour of every day rather than getting sidetracked by low-value or no-value tasks and activities.

Above all, you need the self-discipline to settle in for the long term, to develop a ***long-time perspective*** in your business life. Because of the intensity of competition, it takes many years of disciplined effort for you to become a business success, whether this is in your own business or working for someone else. There are no shortcuts. There are no easy ways to get to the top. There is only one way, and that is through hard work, discipline, and willpower.

On average, it takes about two years to break even in a new business venture. It takes another two years of positive cash flow to pay back the money you borrowed in the first two years. It then takes another three years before you become truly successful. In addition, everything costs twice as much and takes three times as long.

Based on these statistics, why should you start your own business or embark on a new business venture? Because the time is going to pass anyway! After all, five years from now you will be five years older, and ten years from now, you will be ten years older. At the end of that time, you will either be at the top of your field or still down among the 80 percent struggling for every dollar and worrying about money every day. The choice is yours. Discipline is the key.

In the next chapter, you learn the discipline that controls the lifeblood of your business: ***sales***. In the final analysis, as Peter Drucker said, "The purpose of a business is to create and keep a customer."

Action Exercises:

1. Stand back and look at every area of your business, as if you were an outside consultant. What changes would you recommend?
2. Imagine you were starting your business over again today. Are there any products or services that you would not bring to the current market?
3. Identify the 20 percent of your products and services that account for 80 percent of your sales and profits. How could you sell more of them?
4. Project forward one, two, and five years in your business. What are the trends? What will your customers be buying in the future?
5. List three ways you could improve your customer service to ensure that customers buy from you again and tell their friends.
6. List three ways that you could attract more and better qualified leads from your marketing and advertising activities.
7. List three ways that you could make more sales to the prospects you attract or that you could attract more and better prospects.

Chapter 11

Self-Discipline and Sales

"Nothing happens until a sale takes place."
—RED MOTLEY

The most important element in business success is selling. Nothing happens until a sale takes place. All the factories, businesses, offices, and producers of goods and services leap into action only when someone, somewhere makes a sale to someone.

Selling is one of the hardest professions in America. It is also the only profession in which a person can start with limited skills to achieve one of the highest incomes in our economy. Moving onward and upward in sales is like driving on the Autobahn in Germany: There are no speed limits. You can go as far and as fast as you want by stepping on the accelerator of your own ambition and determination to excel in the profession of sales.

• • •

Business Success or Failure

Thousands of bankrupt or insolvent companies have been analyzed over the years to determine why they failed. After all the data was sorted and studied, virtually every business failure came down to one reason: "low sales." In contrast, whenever a business was succeeding, growing, yielding profitability, increasing its share prices, and offering opportunity for more and more people, the reason boiled down to one factor: "high sales." Everything else was secondary.

Almost everything you do in a business either increases or decreases sales. ***Everything*** either helps or hurts. ***Everything*** either attracts and keeps more customers—or drives them away. ***Everything*** counts when it comes to sales.

The Discipline of Generating Sales

Whether you are a salesperson or a business owner, you require the self-discipline to focus and concentrate on generating sales ***every hour*** of ***every business day.***

A group of researchers interviewed several hundred senior executives and business owners and asked them, "How important are sales and marketing to your business?"

Without exception, they all replied, "Sales and marketing are absolutely essential to our survival and growth."

The researchers then conducted a time-and-motion study of these same business owners and executives, following them around and tracking their time usage over the course of a month. At the end of that time, they completed their calculations and determined that the average business owner or executive—who professed that sales were "absolutely essential" to survival and growth—was spending ***only 11 percent*** of his time on sales and marketing. The remaining time was spent on meetings, discussions, paperwork, administrative work, luncheons, and a variety of other activities that contributed ***nothing*** to sales generation.

If you are a sales manager or business owner, you must discipline yourself to focus most of your time and attention on getting your salespeople to generate the sales on which your company depends. You must spend 75 ***percent of your time*** working with your salespeople and accompanying them when they visit your customers to make presentations and sales. Do your paperwork before or after work, but during working hours, when customers are available to be seen, you should dedicate yourself entirely to sales generation.

How to Go Broke

Some years ago, I started a new business. I developed the product and then began advertising via direct mail, radio, television, and newspaper. I allowed myself to become completely overwhelmed with planning, paperwork, and advertising activities. By the end of the year, I was out of money, and my business was almost broke.

At that time, I realized that I had taken my eye off the ball of sales. I then sat down over Christmas and designed a complete sales process. On January 2nd, I picked up the telephone and began making appointments. Over the next two months of aggressive and focused sales activity, I did more business than I had done over the entire previous year. I saved my business—and my home—and I never lost sight of that focus again.

One of the most important questions you can ask as a salesperson, entrepreneur, or business owner is whether what you're doing right now is leading to a sale. Ask this question of yourself repeatedly throughout the day. Every time the answer comes up "no," you must immediately stop whatever you are doing of lower value and turn your attention to sales generation. In addition, make sure that all the people who are responsible for sales in your company ask and answer this question in the affirmative all day long.

Overcome Your Fear of Rejection

Assuming that you have an attractive product or service, one that is reasonably priced and suited to the current market, the biggest problem that telephone salespeople and outside salespeople face is ***rejection***. The fear of rejection does more to sabotage a sales career and undermine sales activities than any other single factor. It is the major obstacle to sales success.

It takes tremendous discipline for salespeople to get up every morning and go out and face the inevitable rejection that they know they are going to receive all day long. Most people cannot handle this continuous rejection. Therefore, to avoid the emotional pain that comes with rejection, many salespeople engage in a series of "displacement" activities to avoid being rejected.

First of all, they make *fewer* calls. According to Columbia University, the average salesperson works about ninety minutes per day—in other words, only about one and a half hours out of an eight-hour day. He spends the rest of the time warming up and getting ready, shuffling paperwork, checking the Internet, reading the newspaper, chatting with coworkers, coming in late, leaving early, and taking extended lunches and coffee breaks. As a result, by the end of the day, on average, ***the salesperson has worked only ninety minutes.***

Increase Face Time with Customers and Prospects

When is a salesperson working? The salesperson is working only when he or she is ear to ear (on the phone) or face to face with someone who can and will buy within a reasonable period of time.

The rule for sales success can be contained in six words: "Spend more time with better prospects." There is no other way to generate a high, consistent, and predictable level of sales results.

Because of the fear of rejection, however, salespeople procrastinate and delay throughout the sales day, doing everything possible to avoid getting face to face with people who can say "no!"

The key to sales success, as I learned as a young salesman, is to realize that ***rejection is not personal.*** Prospective customers always say things like, "No, I'm not interested" or variations of, "I don't want it," "I don't need it," "I can't use it," "I can't afford it," "I'm not in the market right now," or "I'm happy with my existing supplier."

The professional salesperson realizes that these are simply normal and natural responses to any commercial offer in a competitive marketplace. Again, they are ***not*** personal—so don't take them personally.

Remain Positive and Optimistic

The key to sales success is to eliminate the fear of rejection, to become so confident and optimistic that you can call continually all day long and still remain positive and cheerful. As Winston Churchill said, "Success is the ability to go from failure to failure with no loss of enthusiasm."

There is a direct relationship between the number of new customer contacts you make and your level of sales. If you want to increase the number of sales, simply ***discipline yourself to call on more prospects.***

When you increase your levels of sales activity, you also activate the Law of Probabilities to work on your behalf. You tap into the law of averages. You "work the numbers" to ensure success.

How to Double Your Sales Income

Practice the "Minutes Principle" in your sales work. This principle says that, if you are earning all the money that you are earning today with only the number of minutes you are spending face to face with customers today, by increasing that number of minutes, you can also increase your sales.

With outside salespeople, we encourage them to double the number of minutes they spend face to face with customers. We teach them to use every bit of intelligence and creativity they have to increase the amount of time they spend talking in person with prospects rather than following the path of least resistance and allowing themselves to procrastinate getting out into the marketplace.

In almost every case, when a salesperson doubles the number of minutes that he or she spends face to face or ear to ear with customers, that salesperson's sales double as well. This is not an accident. It is based on law: the Law of Probabilities.

Control Your Sales Activities

You can seldom tell where your next sale is going to come from. Therefore, you have to "cast a wide net" and speak to as many prospective customers as possible.

The actual sale itself is not under your direct control. It is controlled by a variety of factors about which you can do very little. But the ***activities*** that lead to sales are completely under your control. The rule is "Do what you can with what you have right where you are."

To achieve high levels of sales success, you must discipline yourself to plan your days and weeks in advance. You must discipline yourself to ***plan*** your sales activities—especially your prospecting activities—every single day, and then you have to discipline yourself to ***follow through*** on your plans and resolutions.

Improve Your Ratios

There are certain ratios in selling that largely determine how many sales you make. These ratios vary depending on your level of experience and ability, the competition, the prices of your products or services, and the general market. Nonetheless, these ratios always exist:

- There is a direct ratio between the number of ***cold calls*** you make and the number of ***prospective customers*** that you will be able to talk to or visit.
- There is a direct ratio between the number of ***prospective customers*** that you see or talk to and the number of ***prospects*** that you can follow up on.
- There is a direct ratio between the number of people you ***follow up on*** with proposals and presentations and the number of sales that you ***close.***

You can also think of this as a "sales funnel":

- Into the funnel—i.e., the broad end—go your prospects.
- The second part of your funnel is your presentations.
- The third part is where you follow up and close the sale.

Keys to Sales Success

You have two responsibilities when it comes to achieving success in sales:

1. ***First of all, keep your funnel full.*** Always have more prospects to call on than you have time during the day. Never let your funnel become empty. *Never* run out of prospects.

2. ***Second, get better at each stage of selling.*** Study, read, listen to audio programs, and upgrade your skills in prospecting, presenting, and closing sales. The better you get, the fewer prospects you require in the top of the funnel to generate sales out of the bottom of the funnel.

Start Early

Discipline yourself to make your first call early in the morning, by 7:00 or 8:00 A.M. When you start your day with a face-to-face sales call, you will be more energized and motivated to continue selling all day long.

Discipline yourself to ***cluster*** your calls in a small geographical area so that you can get face to face with more people in a shorter amount of time. Many salespeople, because of their fear of rejection, spread their calls out over a large geographical area and then convince themselves that they are actually working when they are really simply driving from call to call.

Remember: You are working ***only*** when you are ear to ear or face to face with someone who can and will buy within a reasonable period of time. At all other times, you are "unemployed."

Set Higher Standards for Yourself

Discipline yourself to act every minute of the day as if everyone were watching you. Outside salespeople require a higher level of discipline than people who work in the office where everyone can see them. Because salespeople are on their own, like guerilla fighters in the sales jungle, the temptation is never ending to slack off, to take it easy, or to go for coffee or lunch rather than to make sales calls.

To perform at your best, you must ***discipline*** yourself to work throughout the day—as though your sales manager was doing a "ride-along." Imagine that your sales manager is sitting next to you all day long. How would you work differently if someone were accompanying you and observing everything you did throughout the day? Whatever your answer, that is how you should work—even when no one else is around.

All Sales Skills Are Learnable

To become one of the highest paid salespeople in your industry, you must discipline yourself to practice continuous personal and professional development. Read in your field every day. Listen to educational audio programs in your car as you drive along. Attend every sales seminar you can, whether sponsored by your company or not. Dedicate yourself to continuous learning as if your future depends on it—because it does.

The turning point in my life when I was a young salesman—frustrated and unhappy, going in circles, and barely making a living—was when I learned the Law of Cause and Effect. I learned that "if you do what the most successful salespeople do, over and over, there is nothing that can stop you from eventually achieving the same results and rewards that they do."

I learned that every salesperson in the top 10 percent started in the bottom 10 percent. Everyone who is doing well today was at one time doing poorly. Every person at the top of your field was at one time not in your field at all and did not know that it existed.

I learned that all sales skills are ***learnable***. You can learn any sales skill you need to learn to achieve any sales goal you can set for yourself. There are no limits except the limits you place on yourself with your own thinking.

When you discipline yourself to become one of the top salespeople in your field, you will find that you will have turned an important corner in your career. Most salespeople do only what they have to do to keep their jobs. But those people who resolve to become the best in their fields accomplish far more than anyone else. Your job is to be one of them.

In the next chapter, we will talk about ***money*** and how the practice of self-discipline in this area can dramatically increase your likelihood of achieving all your financial goals.

Action Exercises:

1. See yourself as the president of your own personal sales corporation, completely responsible for sales results. This is the attitude of the highest paid salespeople.
2. Set clear, written income goals for yourself for the next twelve months as well as goals for each month of the year.
3. Determine exactly how much of your product or service you will have to sell in order to earn that desired income.

4. Determine how many individual sales you will have to make, based on your average size of sale and amount of commission earned.
5. Determine how many prospects you will have to call on, based on your current experience, to make this number of sales.
6. Dedicate yourself to continuous improvement in sales by reading each day, listening to audios in your car, and attending sales seminars.
7. Spend every minute of every sales day getting face to face with people who can and will buy from you in the near future.

Chapter 12

Self-Discipline and Money

"In reading the lives of great men, I found that the first victory they won was over themselves; self discipline with all of them came first."
—HARRY S. TRUMAN

According to insurance industry statistics, of one hundred people who start work at age twenty-one, by age sixty-five, one will be rich, four will be financially independent, fifteen will have some money put aside, and the other eighty will be still working, broke, dependent on pensions, or dead.

Most baby boomers today are planning to work into their seventies. Why is this? It is because they don't have enough money put aside so they can stop working.

The primary reason for financial problems in life is lack of self-discipline, self-mastery, and self-control. It is the inability to delay gratification in the short term. It is the tendency for people to spend everything they earn and a little more besides, usually supplemented by loans and credit card debt.

Today, the savings rate in America is too low to achieve financial independence. After a lifetime of work, the average American family has a net worth of only about $8,000. People continue to spend and borrow as if there is no tomorrow.

The good news is that we are living in the most affluent time in all of human history. There are more opportunities to achieve wealth and prosperity today for more people and in more different ways than have ever existed in the history of man. It has never been more possible for you to achieve financial independence than right now. But ***you must make a resolution*** to do it, and then you must follow through on your resolution.

The Reasons for Financial Failure

The primary reason why most adults have financial problems is not low earnings. In their book ***The Millionaire Next Door,*** Thomas Stanley and William Danko show that two families living on the same street, in the same size of house, and working at the same job can have completely different financial situations. By the age of forty-five or fifty, the couple in one house will be financially independent while the couple next door is deeply in debt and having trouble making the minimum payments on their credit cards.

The reason for this is ***not*** the amount of money that they earn. The reason is ***lack of self-discipline*** and the ***inability to delay gratification.*** Why is this weakness of character so prevalent among the majority of adults in society today? It goes back to early childhood.

When you were a child and you received money (whether it was your allowance or a gift from a friend or relative), the first thing you thought of doing was to ***spend*** that money on candy. Candy is sweet. Candy is delicious. Candy fills your mouth with a wonderful, sugary flavor. You liked candy when you were a child, and you probably could seldom get enough of it. Many children will eat candy until they become physically ill because it tastes so good.

As you grew older, you developed what psychologists call a "conditioned response" to receiving money from any source. Like Pavlov's dog, when you receive money, you mentally salivate at the thought of spending this money on something that makes you happy, at least temporarily.

Spending Makes You Happy

When you become an adult and you earn or receive money, this automatic reaction continues. Your first thought is, "How can I spend this money to achieve immediate pleasure?"

When you get your first job, the very first thing you think about is how you can spend not only the money you earn, but also every penny you can borrow on a credit card on clothes, cars, cosmetics, socializing, entertainment, travel, and everything else. Your mental equation is money = enjoyment.

When you go on vacation to a resort of any kind, you find that the hotels and streets are lined with shops selling useless trinkets, bobbles, and trash, plus clothes, artwork, and other items that you would never think of buying at home. Why is this? Simple. When you are on vacation, you feel happy. You have a conditioned response to associate happiness with spending money. The happier you are, the more unconsciously compelled you are to go out and spend money on something—or, rather, on ***anything***.

It is quite common for many people, when they are unhappy or frustrated for any reason, to go shopping. They unconsciously associate buying something with being happy. When it doesn't work as they expected, they buy something else. Sometimes, unhappy people go on shopping sprees. They buy lots of things they don't particularly need because they unconsciously associate spending with happiness.

As an adult, whenever you receive your paycheck, a bonus, a commission, an IRS refund, a prize, or an inheritance, the very first thing you think about is how you can spend this money as quickly as possible and on as many pleasures as possible.

Rewire Your Responses About Money

The starting point of achieving financial independence is to discipline yourself to ***rewire*** your attitude toward money. You need to reach into your subconscious mind and disconnect the wire linking "spending" and "happiness." You need to then reconnect that "happiness" wire to the "saving and investing" wire.

From that moment on, instead of saying, "I feel happy when I spend money," you will say, "I feel happy when I *save* money."

To reinforce this shift in thinking, open up a "financial freedom account" at your local bank. This is the account in which you deposit money for the long term. Once your money goes into this account, you resolve that you will never spend it on anything except the achievement of financial freedom.

If you want to save money to buy a boat or a car, you open up a separate account solely for that purpose. But your financial freedom account is inviolable. You never touch it except to invest those funds so that they can yield a higher rate of return.

Associate Happiness with Saving

When you begin saving in this way, something miraculous happens within you. You start to feel happy about the idea of having money in the bank. Even if you open your account with only $10, this action gives you a feeling of greater self-control and personal power. You feel happier about yourself. The very act of disciplining yourself to save money makes you feel stronger and more in control of your destiny.

Each time you get some extra money, you put it into your financial freedom account. Eventually, your financial freedom account will begin to grow. Then, as it grows, you activate two laws: the Law of Attraction and the Law of Accumulation.

Because the money in your account is ***emotionalized*** by your own thoughts and feelings, it sets up a force field of energy that begins to attract more money into it. If you save $10 a month for a year, you will be astonished to find that with the extra bits of money that you have put into that account, you will probably have more than $200 rather than just $120. If you save $100 per month, you will probably have more than $2,000.

The Law of Accumulation says that "every great achievement is an accumulation of many small achievements." The Law of Attraction says that "you attract into your life those things that are in harmony with your dominant thoughts." Because of these laws, your financial freedom account begins to grow with ***the miracle of compound interest.***

The more money you have in your bank account, the more energy it generates and the more money is attracted into your life. You have heard it said that "it takes money to make money." This is true. As you begin to save and accumulate money, the universe begins to direct more and more money toward you that you can save and accumulate.

Everyone who has ever practiced this principle of regular saving is absolutely astonished at how quickly their financial fortunes change for the better.

The rule for financial independence, once you have rewired your attitude toward money, is to "pay yourself first." Most people save whatever is left over after their monthly expenses—if there is anything left over at all. The key, however, is to pay yourself ***first***, off the top, from every amount of money you receive.

Save Throughout Your Lifetime

It used to be that if you saved 10 percent of your income from your first paycheck until you retired, you would be financially independent, if not rich. Today, however, financial advisers suggest that you need to save ***15 or 20 percent*** of your income in order to achieve all your financial goals. Any less than this opens you up to the risk of running out of money later in life.

When we suggest to people that they need to begin saving 10 percent of their incomes, they shake their heads. Most people are spending everything they earn today. They have nothing left over. Most people are deeply in debt as well. The idea of saving 10 percent of their income, right off the top, appears impossible. But there is a solution.

Practice the 1 Percent Formula

Begin today to save 1 percent of your income and learn to live on the other 99 percent. This is a manageable amount. This is a number that you can get your mind around. It requires only a small amount of self-discipline and delayed gratification for you to save 1 percent each month. If you are earning $3,000 per month, 1 percent is $30 per month, or only $1 per day.

At the end of each day, come home and put your daily amount into a box or jar. Once per month, take your accumulated savings down to the bank and put it into your financial freedom account. This sounds like a small beginning, but remember that "a journey of a thousand leagues begins with a single step."

In no time at all, you will become comfortable living on 99 percent of your income. At that point, you raise your savings level to 2 percent of your income per month. You then adjust your lifestyle to live on 98 percent. In no time, this will become a habit; you will find it automatic and easy to live on 98 percent of what you earn.

Month by month, you then increase your savings level by 1 percent. By the end of the year, you will probably be saving 10 percent of your income. Then something else remarkable will start to happen. Your debts will start to decline. As you become consciously aware of saving your money and moving toward financial independence, you will become more intelligent and thoughtful about each expenditure. You will find yourself spending less and gradually paying off your debts, month by month.

The Payoff Is Tremendous

The reward for saving and investing is substantial. It is said that "happiness is the progressive realization of a worthy ideal." So every time you save a dollar or pay off a dollar of indebtedness, you feel happy inside. You feel more positive and in control of your life. Your brain releases endorphins, which in turn give you a feeling of calmness and well-being.

Within two years of beginning this process, you will have worked your way out of debt and will have begun to accumulate a growing amount of money in your financial freedom account. As this amount increases, you will begin to attract into your life ***more*** money and more opportunities to deploy those funds intelligently so that they yield a higher rate of return.

At the same time, your attitude toward money and spending will gradually change. You will become more disciplined and conscientious. You will investigate carefully before you invest. You will study every aspect of a potential business or opportunity. You will be reluctant to part with money that you have worked so hard to accumulate. You will actually begin to reshape your attitude and personality toward money—and do so in a very positive way.

Income Increases Don't Help

Sometimes I ask my audiences, "Who here would like to be financially independent?" Everybody raises their hand. So then I ask, "If I could wave a magic wand and double the income of every person in this room, would that help you to become financially independent?"

Everybody cheers and laughs and nods their head, agreeing that if they could miraculously double their income, they could become financially independent.

I then ask them, "How many people in this room, from the time you took your first job to today, have already ***doubled*** your income?"

Without hesitation, every hand in the room goes up.

I then ask, "How many people here, from the time you took your first job to today, have increased your income three times? Five times? Ten times?"

Hands go up all over the room. Everyone in the room has doubled or tripled or increased their income five or ten times from the time they took their first job.

I then make my point: "Everyone here has already increased their income dramatically, but it has done no good. Simply increasing your income does not ensure that you will achieve financial independence. This is because of Parkinson's Law, which says, 'Expenditures rise to meet income.' No matter how much you earn, you end up spending it all, and more besides."

Practice the Wedge Principle

The way to achieve financial independence is for you to break Parkinson's Law. You do this by practicing the "Wedge Principle" for the rest of your life. Here is how you do it: As your income increases in the months and years ahead, ***drive a wedge*** between your increasing income and your increasing expenses. Instead of spending it all, resolve that you will save 50 percent of your "increase."

If your income increases by $100 per month, resolve to save $50 per month, off the top, and put it into your financial freedom account. You can spend the other $50 on your family and on improving your lifestyle. But you must resolve to save ***half*** of your increase for the rest of your financial life.

When you pay yourself first, saving 10 or 15 percent of your income off the top and then saving 50 percent of your increase for the rest of your career, you will soon achieve financial independence. You will join the top 5 percent of wealthy people in our society. You will never have to worry about money again.

The Miracle of Compound Interest

Albert Einstein said, "Compound interest is the most powerful force in the universe."

If, from the age of twenty-one until you are sixty-five, you were to save only $100 per month and invest that amount in a mutual fund or index fund that increased an average of 7 to 10 percent per year, you would be worth more than a million dollars. If you were to set up your payroll account so that $100 were automatically deducted and invested for you, you could be sure of becoming one of the wealthiest people in America.

This means that if you are serious about achieving financial independence, the most important single requirement is self-discipline combined with the ability to delay gratification. Your ability to practice self-mastery, self-control, and self-denial throughout your life will not only enable you to achieve all your financial goals, but it will also make you successful and happy in everything else you do.

In the next chapter, we will talk about the key to making almost everything in your life work for you: the use of your ***time***. We all start off in life with lots of time and little money. How you spend your time throughout your adult years largely determines the quality of your life.

Action Exercises:

1. Make a decision today to take complete control of your financial life, get out of debt, and achieve financial independence.
2. Determine your net worth today. Add up all your assets, subtract all your debts and liabilities, and calculate the exact number.
3. Set up a separate bank account and begin saving at least 1 percent of your income as you receive it every month or paycheck.
4. Make a list of all your debts and begin paying them off, starting with those carrying the highest interest rates.
5. Calculate the exact amount that you will need to be financially independent at the end of your career and then set this as a goal.
6. Set specific financial accumulation goals for yourself for each month, quarter, and year for the rest of your life.
7. Practice frugality in spending by putting off and delaying every expenditure you possibly can until you achieve your long-term financial goals.

Chapter 13

Self-Discipline and Time Management

"If you do not conquer self, you will be conquered by self."
—Napoleon Hill

There is perhaps no area of your life in which self-discipline is more important than in the way you manage your time. Time management is a core discipline that largely determines the quality of your life. As Peter Drucker said, "You cannot manage time; you can only manage yourself."

Time management is really ***life*** management, personal management, management of yourself rather than of time or circumstances.

Time is perishable; it cannot be saved. Time is irreplaceable; nothing else will do. Time is irretrievable; once it is gone or wasted, you can never get it back. Finally, time is indispensable, especially for accomplishments of any kind. All achievement, all results, all success requires time.

You Can't "Save" Time

The fact is that you cannot ***save*** time; you can only ***spend*** it differently. You can only reallocate your time usage from areas of low value to areas of high value. Herein lies the key to success, and the requirement for self-discipline.

Time management is the ability to choose the ***sequence of events***. By exerting your self-discipline with regard to time, you can choose what to do first, second, and not at all. And you are always free to choose.

You require tremendous self-discipline to overcome the procrastination and delay that holds most people back from great success. A native Indian once told me that "procrastination is the thief of dreams."

The Pareto Principle, the 80/20 rule, says that 20 percent of the things you do account for 80 percent of the value of what you accomplish. This means that 80 percent of what you do is worth 20 percent or less of the value of what you accomplish.

Assess the True Value of Everything You Do

Some things you do are five times and even ten times more valuable than other things, even though they take the same number of minutes and hours. The most important things you do—the top 20 percent—are usually big, difficult, and daunting. In contrast, the 80 percent of things that you do that make little or no difference to your life are usually fun, easy, and enjoyable.

You can tell the value that something has to you by the amount of your time you invest in it. You always pay attention to and spend time on what you most value, whether it is your family, your health, your social or sports activities, or your money and career. It is only by looking at how you spend your time that you (and everyone else) know what is really important to you.

Some people say that career success is most important to them, and then they go home and watch television several hours per day. Some people say their families are important to them, and then they go out socializing or playing golf. Only your ***actions*** tell you—and others—what you truly value.

The essence of time management is for you to discipline yourself to set clear priorities—and then ***stick to those priorities.*** You must consciously and deliberately select the most valuable and important thing that you could be doing at any given time, and then discipline yourself to work solely on that task.

Personal Strategic Planning

In corporate strategic planning, the main focus is on increasing the "return on equity." Equity in a business is defined as the amount of money invested in the business by the owners (aside from debt and money borrowed). The purpose of strategic planning is to find ways to organize and reorganize the business in such a way that the company is achieving a higher rate of return on this equity than it would be in the absence of the planning process.

Companies invest financial capital, but individuals invest "human capital." Companies deploy financial assets, but ***your*** most vital assets are your mental, emotional, and physical energies. How you invest them determines your entire quality of life.

In personal strategic planning, your goal is to get the highest "return on energy" from your activities. Ken Blanchard refers to this as getting the highest "return on life."

Just as you would be careful about investing your money so as to ensure that you get the highest rate of return, you must be equally careful when you invest your time. You must be sure that you earn the highest level of results, rewards, and satisfaction from the limited amount of time you have.

Think Before You Act

Before you commit to any time-consuming activity, you must always ask, "Is this the very best use of my time?"

Lack of self-discipline in time management leads people to procrastinate their top tasks continually, causing them to spend more and more time on tasks of low or no value. And whatever you do repeatedly eventually becomes a habit.

Many people have developed the habit of procrastination, of putting off their major tasks and instead spending most of their time on activities that make very little difference in the long run.

Priorities versus Posteriorities

Setting priorities requires setting ***posteriorities*** as well. A priority is something that you do more of and sooner, whereas a posteriority is something you do less of or later. You are probably already overwhelmed with too much to do and too little time. Because of this, for you to embark on a new task, you must ***discontinue*** an old task. Getting into something new requires getting out of another activity. Before you commit to a new undertaking, ask yourself, "What am I going to ***stop*** doing so that I have enough time to work on this new task?"

Go through your life regularly and practice "creative abandonment": Consciously determine the activities that you are going to ***discontinue*** so that you have more time to spend on those tasks that can ***really make a difference*** to your future.

Identify the Consequences

One of the most important words in developing the discipline of time management is "consequences." Something is important to the degree that it has serious ***potential*** consequences for completion or noncompletion. A task or activity is unimportant to the degree that it does not matter if it is done or not.

For example, completing a course of study at the university can have enormous consequences that can impact your life for the next fifty years. Completing a major task or project at work or making an important sale can have significant consequences for your job and your income.

On the other hand, drinking coffee, chatting with coworkers, reading the newspaper, surfing the Internet, or checking emails may be enjoyable, but these activities have few or no consequences. In other words, whether you do them or not makes little to no difference to your work or your life. However, it is precisely on these activities that most people spend most of their time.

Managing Your Time

There is a simple time management system that you can use to overcome procrastination. It requires self-discipline, willpower, and personal organization, but the payoff is huge. When you use this system, you can double or even triple your productivity, performance, output, and income.

Before you begin each day, start by making a list of everything you have to do that day. The best time to make this list is the evening before, at the end of the workday, so that your subconscious mind can work on your list of activities while you sleep. You will often wake up with ideas and insights for how to more effectively complete the tasks of the day.

Then apply the A B C D E Method to your list:

- A = "Must do"—Serious consequences for noncompletion;
- B = "Should do"—Mild consequences for doing or not doing;
- C = "Nice to do"—No consequences whether you do it or not;

- D = "Delegate"—Everything you possibly can to free up more time for those things that only you can do;
- E = "Eliminate"—Discontinue all tasks and activities that are no longer essential to your work and to achieving your goals.

Review your list of activities for the coming day and write an A, B, C, D, or E next to each task before you start.

If you have several "A" tasks, rank them by importance by writing A-1, A-2, A-3, and so on. Do this with your B and C tasks as well.

The rule is that you should never do a B task when you have an A task left undone. You should never do a lower-value task when you have a higher-value task before you.

Once you have organized your list using this system, discipline yourself to start on your A-1 task first thing in the morning, before you do anything else.

Practice Single-Handling

Once you have begun work on your most important task, you must discipline yourself to concentrate single-mindedly, with 100 percent of your time and attention, until that task is complete.

It takes tremendous self-discipline to select your most important task and then to start on that task rather than doing anything else. But once you begin to work on it, you will start to feel a flow of energy that motivates and propels you into the task. You will feel more positive and confident. You will feel happier and more determined.

The very act of starting on an important task raises your self-esteem and motivates you to continue.

Deep within each person is an intense desire to feel strong, effective, powerful, and in control of his or her life. You automatically trigger these feelings of self-confidence and self-esteem when you discipline yourself to start work on the task that is most important to you at the moment.

1,000 Percent Return on Investment

This A B C D E Method seldom takes more than about ten minutes to organize your entire day. But you will save ten minutes in execution for every minute that you invest in this way of planning before you begin.

This means that you will get a 1,000 percent "return on energy" from the act of planning thoroughly and setting clear priorities before you start on your first task.

As you feel yourself moving forward, making progress on your most important task, your brain releases a steady flow of endorphins, nature's "happy drug." These endorphins will make you feel more positive, focused, alert, aware, and in control.

When you discipline yourself to push against your natural resistance to get started on your most important task, you get an "endorphin rush." You experience this as a sense of elation, exhilaration, happiness, and high self-esteem. By completing a major task, you feel exactly like an athlete who has crossed the finish line first. You feel like a ***winner.***

Your payoff from excellent time management is never ending. As soon as you begin to plan and organize your time, set priorities, and begin on your A-1 task, you will feel happy and more in control of yourself and your life. The better you plan and execute, the better you feel.

Keep Yourself Focused

The Law of Forced Efficiency says, "There is never enough time to do *everything,* but there is always enough time to do the *most important* things."

Here are some questions that you should ask yourself, to help keep you focused and working on your top tasks, activities, and responsibilities:

1. *Why am I on the payroll? Exactly what have I been hired to do? What results are expected of me?*

You must be clear about your answer to this question. Discuss it with others. Ask your boss.

2. *What are my key result areas? Of all the things I do, what are the most important results that I am expected to achieve in my position?*

There are seldom more than five to seven key result areas in any job. It is essential that you identify yours and then work in those areas all day long.

3. *What are my highest value activities? Of all the things I do, which activities contribute the greatest value to my company and to myself?*

You have core competencies that enable you to make a valuable contribution. What are they?

4. ***What can I—and only I—do, that if done well, will make a real difference?***

There is only one answer to this question at any given time. This is something that you ***and only you*** can do. If you don't do it, no one else will do it instead. But if you do it—and you do it well—it can make a tremendous difference in your life and work.

5. ***What is the most valuable use of my time right now?***

This is the most important of all questions for setting priorities and overcoming procrastination. At every minute of every day, there is an answer to this question. Your ability to organize your life and to select your highest priority is a key measure of your intelligence and your effectiveness.

Start Today

Starting today, you should apply these key time management principles to every area of your life. Apply them to your work, family, health, exercise routine, and financial decisions and activities. No excuses.

You require tremendous discipline to set priorities and then stick to those priorities. You require the continuous exertion of discipline and willpower to overcome the procrastination that holds most people back. However, the more you discipline yourself to use your time well, the happier you will feel and the better will be the quality of your life in every area.

What stands between you and your goals are almost always ***problems*** and ***difficulties*** of some kind. Your ability to effectively solve the problems of daily life can have an enormous impact on your results and rewards. We will talk about this in the next chapter.

Action Exercises:

1. Make a decision today to become absolutely excellent at time management. Work at it until it becomes a habit.
2. Before you begin each day, make a list of everything you have to do that day. As new tasks arise, write them down before you act on them.
3. Organize your work list by priority by using the A B C D E Method over and over until it becomes a habit.
4. Identify your A-1 task each day and resolve to work single-mindedly on that task until it is totally complete.
5. Identify the one task that *only you* can do and that, if you do it well, can make a real difference.
6. Determine the 20 percent of your tasks that can account for 80 percent of your results, and then discipline yourself to work on them most of the time.
7. Every minute of every day, ask yourself, "What is the most valuable use of my time, right now?" and then discipline yourself to work on *only* that task until it is complete.

Chapter 14

Self-Discipline and Problem Solving

*"Experience is not what happens to a man;
it is what a man does with what happens to him."*
—Aldous Huxley

Thoughts are causes and conditions are effects. Therefore, the quality of your thinking largely determines the quality of your life. The greatest mental principle is that "you become what you think about most of the time."

Top people in every field are intensively ***solution-oriented***. They think about solutions most of the time. Instead of getting bogged down in who did or didn't do something or other, the most successful people in every field concentrate on the solutions and what can be done to solve the problem.

The Sufi philosopher Izrhat Khan once said, "Life is a continuous succession of problems, like waves from the ocean. They never stop." This means that your ability to practice self-discipline, self-mastery, and self-control when faced with the never-ending flow of problems, difficulties, setbacks, and temporary failures you will experience is essential to your success in business and in life.

The Inevitable and Unavoidable Crisis

Throughout your life, you will face a river of problems—physical, financial, family, business, and political. The only break in this never-ending chain of problems will be the occasional *crisis*. If you are living a normal life, you will probably experience a crisis every two or three months. And it is in these crises that you truly demonstrate the quality of your personality and the strength of your character.

It is only when you face unexpected reversals and setbacks that you show the world what you are truly made of. All of life is a "test." The only question for you is do you pass or fail?

By their very nature, crises come "unbidden." You have no warning or ability to anticipate them in advance. If you did, it wouldn't be a crisis in the first place—obviously, or you would already be prepared. When the inevitable crisis occurs, more than at any other time, self-discipline is required so you can remain calm and clear-headed in order to deal with the crisis effectively.

Perform at Your Best

When something goes wrong, the natural tendency of most people is to become angry and look around for someone to blame. But this is a waste of energy. It solves nothing. Instead, you must discipline yourself to remain calm, objective, and unemotional.

When you face an unexpected problem or crisis, discipline yourself to stay calm, to focus on the solution rather than the problem. Think in terms of ***what can be done now***, rather than thinking about how it occurred and who is to blame.

Like an accident where someone is hurt, you focus on caring for the injured person, stopping the bleeding, and minimizing the damage before you start analyzing what and how it happened. Practice self-discipline when dealing with a problem or crisis by immediately saying, "I am responsible," even if, at that moment, you are responsible only for controlling your responses.

Keep Your Mind Clear

Top people have developed the ability to respond effectively to a crisis, to remain calm, relaxed, and clear-eyed. They discipline themselves to stay cool and unemotional. This enables them to think more clearly, to analyze the situation objectively, and to make better decisions.

But the moment you become angry and upset, your neocortex—or your "thinking brain"—shuts down. All you have left then is your paleocortex, your ***emotional*** brain, which thinks in terms of "fight or flight." When your emotional brain is in charge, you think in terms of black and white, yes or no, or doing something or doing nothing. You lose the ability to think in shades of gray and to look at all the different possible ways to deal with this particular situation.

Top people realize that every problem is an opportunity to grow in self-control and personal confidence. In fact, you will rise in life to the height of the problems that you are capable of solving.

Stepping Stones to Success

Some years ago, Dr. Lawrence Peter wrote a book called ***The Peter Principle.*** It was an amusing book with a central thesis that cut too close to home. He wrote that in every organization, people continue to be promoted until they reach a level where they are no longer competent to solve the problems at that level. This is where they stop and stay for the rest of their careers.

Furthermore, he pointed out that for this reason, every organization is eventually staffed by people who have reached their ***level of incompetence.*** This is especially true in government, and it is the primary reason why government is so time- and cost-inefficient, making it difficult to get anything done at all. This is usually true in any large bureaucracy.

In your own personal life, you continue to rise in your company and your profession in direct proportion to your ability to solve the problems and make the necessary decisions at each level of your career. The good news is that when you think about solutions most of the time, you train your brain to be intensively solution oriented.

No matter what problems or difficulties arise around you, your brain will be continually seeking creative ways to solve the problem. As a result, you actually become smarter and quicker, with more of your thinking brain available to you faster.

If you want to learn a physical sport, you begin by learning the basic moves and then the more advanced moves. You practice these skills over and over again until you can perform them and go through the motions naturally and easily every time.

To master the discipline of problem solving, you need to develop a formula or method that enables you to deal effectively with almost any problem you face in the course of your career or personal life. Fortunately, there is a proven formula for problem solving and decision making that you can use in almost any situation. Let's take a look.

A Nine-Step Method for Solving Problems Effectively

Step 1: Take the Time to Define the Problem Clearly. In medicine, they say that "accurate diagnosis is half the cure." Therefore, you need to ask, "What *exactly* is the problem?" It is absolutely amazing how several people can become upset about a problem in an organization, but every one of them has a different idea or definition of the exact nature of the problem they're facing. Your job is to achieve clarity and to get everyone to agree on the definition of the problem *before* you move on to the business of solving it.

Step 2: Ask, "Is It Really a Problem?" Remember, there are some things that you can do nothing about. They're not problems; they are merely ***facts of life***. If interest rates rise or the subprime mortgage market collapses, this is not a problem. It is not something that is amenable to a solution. Instead, it is something that must be worked around and dealt with.

Also, very often what ***appears*** to be a problem or a setback is actually an ***opportunity in disguise***. Sometimes, the problem does not need to be solved at all. Instead, you are now free to do something ***completely different***—which might be even better for you and your organization.

Step 3: Ask, "What Else Is the Problem?" Beware of any problem for which there is only one definition. The more ways you can define a problem, the more likely it is that you will find the best solution.

When we work with corporations in which sales are below a desired level, we force them to ask twenty-one questions, all of which are different ways of restating the problem. Each restatement of the problem, if accepted as the correct definition, leads to a different solution and often to a completely different direction for the organization.

For example, we will ask, "What is the problem?" and the first answer is "Our sales are too low."

The next question is "What else is the problem?"

Answer: "Our competitor's sales are too high."

Notice the difference. If the problem is that your sales are too low, the solution may be to increase your advertising and promotion and beef up your sales activities. If the definition is that your competitor's sales are too high, the answer may be to improve your products, change your product line, lower your prices, or go into a completely different business altogether.

By asking and answering a series of questions like this, we eventually find the correct definition, one that is amenable to a workable solution.

Step 4: Ask, "How Did This Problem Occur?" Seek to understand the causes of the problem so you can ensure that it doesn't happen again. In your life or business, if a problem recurs repeatedly, it is a sign that your business is poorly organized or out of control in that area. There is a defect built into your ***systems*** that is causing the ***same*** problem to recur. Your job is to find out why this happens repeatedly so you can solve the problem at its root.

Step 5: Ask, "What Are All the Possible Solutions?" The more possible solutions you develop, the more likely you will come up with the right one. The ***quality*** of the solution seems to be in direct proportion to the ***quantity*** of solutions considered in problem solving. Beware a problem for which there is ***only one*** solution.

Step 6: Ask, "What Is the Best Solution at This Time?" Sometimes, ***any*** solution is better than ***no*** solution. An average solution vigorously executed is often superior to an excellent solution that cannot be implemented because of its complexity or because no one has the ability to execute it.

The rule is that fully 80 percent of all problems should be dealt with immediately. Only 20 percent of problems need to be put off to a later time. If you must put off a problem, set a specific deadline for making a decision on that problem, and then make your decision at that deadline with whatever information you have at that time.

There is a rule that says that every large problem was once a small problem that could have been solved easily and inexpensively at that time. Sometimes, the best strategy is to "nip it in the bud." When it is clear that there is a problem and a solution, do what has to be done—and do it quickly.

Step 7: Make a Decision. Select a solution, any solution, and then decide on a course of action. Always ask, "What is our next action? What are we going to do ***now***?"

Step 8: Assign Responsibility. Who exactly is going to carry out the solution or the different elements of the solution? It is quite common for a group to meet to solve a problem and to agree on a solution, but when the group meets again two weeks later, it turns out that nothing has happened. Why? No one was made specifically responsible for carrying out the decision.

Step 9: Set a Measure for the Decision. What are you trying to accomplish with this decision, and how will you measure results? How will you know that it worked? The more accurately you can determine the result that you want to achieve by the solution, the more likely it is that you will achieve it.

The Big Reward

The main reward you get for solving problems is the opportunity to solve bigger and more important problems. Your rate of pay and speed of promotion and therefore your forward movement in your career are largely determined by your problem-solving ability. The more you focus on solutions, the more solutions you will come up with, and the more valuable your contribution will be to your organization.

The flip side of self-esteem is called "self-efficacy." Your level of self-efficacy is defined as "how competent you feel you are to solve your problems and achieve your goals."

The more competent you feel you are to solve the problems and difficulties of daily life, the more you like yourself. The more you like yourself, the more confident and competent you become in solving even larger problems and getting even more important results.

The Determinant of Your Success

In your work, your problem-solving ability largely determines everything you accomplish. People who are good at solving problems are some of the most valuable and respected people in every area. For this reason, success has been defined as "the ability to solve problems." This also means that happiness is the ability to solve problems. Leadership is the ability to solve problems.

When you practice self-discipline and self-control in face of the inevitable and unavoidable problems and crises of day-to-day life, you become more competent and effective in everything you do. You will be respected and esteemed by everyone around you. You will experience a tremendous feeling of personal power and competence. In no time at all, you will become one of the most valuable people in your organization.

Action Exercises:

1. Solving problems is like solving mathematical equations: It is learnable with practice and repetition. Start by determining the biggest problems facing you ***today***.
2. Accept complete responsibility for solving the problems you encounter in your daily work, and then think about the ***solutions***.
3. Define your biggest business or personal problem clearly. Write it down. What ***exactly*** is the problem?
4. ***Why*** is this a problem? Could it be an opportunity in disguise? If so, what opportunity or lesson could this problem contain?
5. What ***else*** is the problem? Perhaps the real problem is something else, something you might not want to face?
6. What are ***all*** the possible solutions? What ***else*** could be a solution?
7. Select the best solution that is available to you ***right now***, and take action immediately.

PART III

Self-Discipline and the Good Life

Your ultimate goal in life is to achieve your own happiness. No one else can do this for you. This personal desire is the motivation behind almost every behavior. Moreover, happiness is more emotional and spiritual than it is a matter of acquiring material things. In this part, you will learn how the practice of discipline in the most important areas of your life can bring you more joy and satisfaction than perhaps any other quality.

Chapter 15

Self-Discipline and Happiness

"No horse gets anywhere until he is harnessed. No stream or gas drives anything until it is confined. No Niagara is ever turned into light and power until it is tunneled. No life ever grows great until it is focused, dedicated, disciplined."

—HARRY EMERSON FOSDICK

Your ability to achieve your own happiness is the true measure of your success in life. Nothing is more important. Nothing can replace it. If you accomplish everything of a material nature, but you are not happy, you have actually ***failed*** at fulfilling your potential as a human being.

In Chapter 4, I described how human beings are purposeful, striving toward achieving goals and end results. However, behind each goal lies another goal, and then still another goal, until you finally arrive at the "primum movum," or first-moving force, in human life. This always turns out to be ***the desire to be happy***. You can only truly be happy when you practice self-discipline, self-mastery, and self-control. It is only when you feel that you are in complete control of your life that you are truly content.

The Law of Control

In my book ***Maximum Achievement***, I teach the importance of the Law of Control, which states, "You feel happy to the degree to which you feel you are in control of your own life. You feel unhappy to the degree to which you feel you are ***not*** in control, or controlled by other factors or people."

Psychologists call this your "locus of control." There are fifty years of research and hundreds of books and articles on this subject. They all conclude that stress and unhappiness arise when you feel controlled by outside circumstances. This is explained as the difference between an "internal locus of control" (happy) and an "external locus of control" (unhappy).

You have an ***internal*** locus of control when you feel that you are in charge, you make your own decisions, and what happens to you in life is largely determined by yourself. When you have an internal locus of control, you feel that you are behind the wheel of your own life and that you are in the driver's seat. You feel that you determine most of what happens to you. As a result, you feel strong, purposeful, and happy.

On the other hand, you have an ***external*** locus of control to the degree to which you feel that you are not in control or that you have little ability to direct your own life. For example, if you feel that you are controlled by an arbitrary or critical boss, but you cannot afford to lose your job because you have no savings put aside, you experience high levels of stress and anxiety. This causes you to do a poor job, which makes it even more likely that your difficult boss will fire you, and this very often brings about exactly the circumstances you fear.

Another example is that you may feel you are controlled by a bad marriage or relationship from which you cannot escape. You may feel controlled by your bills, by the money you owe, and your obligations to maintain your standard of living. You may feel that you are controlled by your physical condition or lack of education. Many people feel that they are controlled by their past because of a difficult childhood or upbringing and that there is nothing they can do to change their situation.

Many people feel that they are controlled by their own personalities and that they are not able to change for the better. They say, "That's just the way I am." By saying this, they absolve themselves of all responsibility for exerting the necessary discipline and willpower to make the changes they know they need to make in order to live the kind of life they want to live and to be happy.

The key to replacing an ***external*** locus of control with an ***internal*** locus of control is for you to decide ***today*** to take complete charge of your life. Realize and accept that you make your own decisions and that you are where you are and what you are because of yourself. If there is some area in your life in which you are not happy, discipline yourself to do whatever it takes to change the situation.

The Reason for Happiness

It is often the size of the *gap* between your present situation and the conditions and circumstances that you feel that you need to be happy that determines whether you are happy or unhappy. This is very much a matter of your own evaluation and decision.

There is an old saying that "success is getting what you want; happiness is wanting what you get." When your income and your life are consistent with your goals and expectations and you are content with your situation, you feel happy. If, on the other hand, for any reason your current situation is different from what you really want and expect, you will be discontented and unhappy.

This state of contentment can be constantly changing. When you start off in your career, an income of $50,000 per year can seem like a huge achievement. But once you reach this goal, you start to be unhappy because you are not earning $100,000 or more. Some people are unhappy earning a million dollars a year.

Happiness Is a By-Product

The interesting thing about happiness is that it is not a goal that you can aim at and achieve in and of itself. Happiness is a ***by-product*** that comes to you when you are engaged in doing something that you really enjoy while in the company of people who you like and respect.

Earl Nightingale, perhaps the most famous and respected radio commentator on success in history, said that "happiness is the progressive realization of a worthy ideal." Whenever you feel that you are moving, step-by-step, toward something that is important to you, toward your most important goals, you automatically feel happy. You feel satisfied and content. You feel a tremendous sense of personal growth and well-being.

Five Ingredients of Happiness

Self-discipline is essential to happiness. Self-discipline requires both that you determine clearly what happiness means to you and also that you work progressively each day toward the achievement of that ideal condition.

In my experience and teachings, I have found that there are *five* ingredients to happiness. A shortfall in any of these areas can cause stress, unhappiness, and a feeling of being out of control.

Five Ingredients of Happiness

1. Health and energy. This is perhaps the most important element of a good life. We strive for it all our lives. It is only when you enjoy high levels of pain-free health and a continuous flow of energy that you feel truly happy.

In many cases, health is a "deficiency need." This means that you do not think about your health very much until you are ***deprived*** of it. For example, you do not think about your teeth until you have a toothache. You do not think about your body until you have aches or pains of some kind.

You must use discipline and willpower throughout your life to achieve and maintain high levels of health and fitness. Chapters 16 and 17 cover these in more detail.

2. *Happy relationships.* Fully 85 percent of your happiness—or unhappiness—will come from your relationships with other people. As Aristotle said, "Man is a social animal." We are designed to function in society, working and living with other people at every stage of our lives.

Your ability to enter into and maintain high-quality relationships with your spouse, children, friends, colleagues, and others is the true measure of the quality of your personality and your level of mental health. People with high levels of self-esteem and self-respect get along better with others and have much happier lives.

One of our biggest mistakes is to take our relationships for granted, especially our most important ones. We often don't think about them until there is a problem, and then we think of nothing else.

3. *Meaningful work.* To be truly happy, you must be fully engaged with life. You must be doing things that keep you active and give you a sense of fulfillment. If you are making a living, you must be doing work that you enjoy, do well, and for which you are well paid.

People are truly happy only when they feel they are making a ***contribution*** of some kind, that they are putting in more than they are taking out. You need to feel that what you do really makes a difference in the lives and work of other people.

In studies of employee motivation, employers think that people are primarily motivated by money and benefits. But when employees are surveyed, the three factors that motivate them the most turn out to be

challenging and interesting work;
opportunities for growth and advancement; and
pleasant coworkers.

One of your most important responsibilities to yourself is to find the right job for you, and then, once you have it, throw your whole heart into it. If for any reason, you do not feel like putting your whole heart into your work, it may be lacking one or more of the three essentials to a positive workplace. It may be a sign that this is not the right place for you.

*4. **Financial independence.*** Some of the greatest fears we experience are those of loss, failure, and poverty. We fear being destitute, without funds, and dependent on others.

One of your chief responsibilities to yourself is to work toward financial independence and financial freedom throughout your life. The happiest of all people are those who have reached the point at which they no longer worry about money. This is not something you can leave to chance, but rather something that requires deliberate, purposeful action and tremendous self-discipline to achieve.

Whenever you feel that there is a big gap between where you are today financially and where you would ideally like to be, you experience stress, worry, and unhappiness.

5. Self-actualization. This is the feeling that you are becoming everything you are capable of becoming. This occurs when you feel that you are realizing more and more of your true potential.

Abraham Maslow is best known for his Hierarchy of Needs. He determined that people have both "deficiency needs" and "being needs." People strive either to compensate for their deficiencies or to realize their potentials. He concluded that you begin to evolve and develop to the highest levels possible for you only when your deficiency needs are first satisfied.

Deficiency Needs. Your first deficiency need is for ***safety*** and ***survival.*** Satisfying this need requires that you have sufficient food, water, clothing, and accommodation to preserve your life and well-being. If for any reason your safety or survival is threatened, you will become totally preoccupied with satisfying this need. You will experience tremendous stress, and you will be completely unhappy until you are safe once more. For example, think about being in a life-threatening situation.

The second deficiency need that Maslow identified is the need for ***security***. This need embraces financial, emotional, and physical security. You need to have enough money to provide for yourself, security in your relationships at work and at home, and physical security to assure that you are not in danger of any kind. If your security needs are threatened, you become completely preoccupied with them. For example, think about losing your job suddenly: How would you feel?

The third deficiency need that Maslow identified is ***belongingness***. Each person has a need to be in social relationships with others, both at home and at work. You need to be recognized and accepted by other people in your world. Each person needs to be comfortable in his or her relationships with others and seen and accepted as part of a team or group.

Self-Esteem Needs. Once you have achieved a sufficient level of each of these basic needs—safety, security, and belongingness—you then turn to satisfy the ***higher*** needs for self-esteem and self-worth, your ***being*** needs. Your self-esteem is the core of your personality and largely determines how you feel about everything that happens to you. Everything you do in life is either to increase your self-esteem or to protect it from being diminished.

Your self-esteem—how you ***feel*** about yourself and how much you like and value yourself—determines your happiness more than any other single factor. Your self-esteem comes from many factors. When you are liked and accepted by others, living consistently with your highest values, doing a good job and being recognized for it, and moving progressively toward the achievement of your goals and ideals, then you naturally feel happy and satisfied. You feel valuable and very much in control.

The Highest Human Need. The highest need that Maslow identified was for ***self-actualization***. He concluded that less than 2 percent of the population ever reaches this height of personal fulfillment. Most people remain so preoccupied with their deficiency needs and protecting or enhancing their self-esteem and their ego needs that they give little thought or effort to self-actualization.

But it is only when you realize that you have tremendous personal potential and begin striving to do, be, and have more than ever before in some area that you begin to experience self-actualization and true happiness.

The happiest of all people are those who feel that they are doing something worthwhile and important with their lives. They feel they are ***stretching*** and moving beyond anything they've ever done before. People devoted to self-actualization may be writing books or creating works of art. They may be climbing mountains or competing in sports. They may be building businesses or scaling the heights of their professions.

The wonderful thing about self-actualization needs is that they can never be completely satisfied. As you continually strive throughout your life to be and have and do more than ever before, you experience a steady flow of happiness and contentment. You feel that you are becoming more and more of what you were truly meant to become.

Never Be Satisfied

In each of these areas, whenever you exert self-discipline and willpower to overcome the tendency to take the easy way, you feel happier about yourself. When you take a leap of faith in the direction of your dreams and then discipline yourself to keep going in spite of all obstacles and hardships, you feel powerful. Your self-esteem and self-confidence increase, and then as you move, step by step, toward your ideals, you feel genuinely happy.

In the next chapter, you will learn how to incorporate self-discipline into your daily ***health habits*** to ensure that you live a long, happy, healthy life.

Action Exercises:

1. Identify the areas of your life in which you feel the happiest and the most in control. How could you expand them?
2. Identify the areas of your life in which you feel controlled by other people or factors. What could you do to resolve these situations?
3. Identify those areas in your life in which there is a gap between your current levels of accomplishment and what you would really like to achieve. What could you do to bridge these gaps?
4. Identify the most pressing needs you have today that are not being fulfilled. How could you begin to satisfy these deficiency needs?
5. Identify those activities that give you the greatest feeling of personal happiness, your "peak experiences" in life. What could you do to increase these moments of happiness?
6. Identify those areas in life in which you feel the most discontented. What steps could you take immediately to resolve these feelings of discontent?
7. Define "happiness" for yourself. What does it mean? What would have to happen for you to feel truly happy? What could you do immediately to create this situation?

Chapter 16

Self-Discipline and Personal Health

"Self respect is the root of discipline;
the sense of dignity grows
with the ability to say no to oneself."
—Abraham Joshua Heschel

More people are living longer and better today than ever before in human history, and your goal should be to be one of those people. There is no area in which self-discipline is more important than in your practices regarding your health. Your number one goal for yourself should be to live as long and as well as you possibly can. This requires lifelong self-discipline with your health habits—and as mentioned in Chapter 15, good health is one of the ingredients of overall happiness.

The average life expectancy for males today (in 2009) is 76.8 years; for females 79.8 years, or approximately eighty years, and this number is increasing each year. This means that about 50 percent of the population will die before the age of eighty and about 50 percent will die after the age of eighty. Your goal should be to defy the averages and live to age ninety, ninety-five, or even longer.

Living a Long Life

Today, most causes of early death that had shortened life in the past have been eliminated in the industrialized world. Diseases such as tuberculosis, polio, malaria, cholera, typhus, and others have been wiped out through sanitation and modern medicine.

The predominant causes of early deaths today are heart disease, cancer of all kinds, diabetes, and traffic deaths, all of which are subject to your control to a certain extent.

You cannot predict or protect against the unpredictable, like random accidents, but you can use your self-discipline to control the controllable in your life.

Seven Key Health Habits

The Alameda Study, covering many thousands of people for more than twenty years, concluded there were seven key health habits that contributed the most to long life:

1. ***Eat regularly*** rather than fasting, starving, or gorging. Eat normal, healthy meals, preferably five or six times per day, with your last meal fully three hours before you go to sleep.

2. ***Eat lightly:*** Overeating makes you tired and sluggish, whereas eating lightly makes you feel healthy and alert. As Thomas Jefferson wrote, "No one ever regretted eating too little after a meal."
3. ***Don't snack between meals:*** When you eat, your body has to break down and digest the foods in your stomach so that they can move into your small intestine. This requires four to five hours. If you put food in on top of food that you have already eaten, the digestive process must start over again, with part of your food at one stage of digestion and another part of your food at another stage. This leads to upset stomach, heartburn, drowsiness (especially in the afternoon), and constipation.
4. ***Exercise regularly:*** The ideal is about thirty minutes a day, or two hundred minutes per week. You can achieve this by walking, running, swimming, and/or using exercise equipment. You should fully articulate every joint every day.
5. ***Wear a seatbelt:*** Right up to age thirty-five, the most common cause of premature death is traffic accidents.
6. ***Don't smoke:*** Smoking is correlated with thirty-two different illnesses including lung cancer, esophageal cancer, throat cancer, stomach cancer, heart disease and a variety of other ailments.
7. ***Drink alcohol in moderation:*** Studies show that one to two glasses of wine per day aid digestion

and seem to be beneficial to your overall health. Anything in excess of that can lead to all kinds of problems, including overeating, traffic accidents, personality problems, and antisocial behavior.

Each of these seven factors that contribute to long life are completely a matter of self-discipline. These seven factors are a matter of choice. They are actions that you can choose to take or not take deliberately. They are completely under your control.

The Five Ps of Excellent Health

In my personal development seminars, we teach the five "Ps" of excellent health:

1. Proper weight: This requires the regular exercise of discipline and willpower in order to achieve your proper weight and then to maintain it throughout your life, but the payoff is tremendous. You look good, feel good, and generally feel more positive and in control of your life.

2. Proper diet: As Benjamin Franklin said, "Eat to live, rather than live to eat." According to studies of Olympic athletes from more than 120 countries, the three factors their diets have in common are

1. lean-source protein;
2. a wide variety of fruits and vegetables; and
3. lots of water, about eight glasses per day.

When you begin this "Olympic diet," you will feel more alert, awake, and aware all day long.

*3. **Proper exercise:*** The most important exercise for long life is ***aerobic*** exercise. This requires that you get your heart rate up to a high level for thirty to sixty minutes three times per week. You can achieve this through brisk walking, running, cycling, swimming, or cross-country skiing.

Exercise physiologists have determined that the "exercise effect" clicks in at about twenty-five minutes of vigorous exercise. At this point, your brain releases endorphins that give you a feeling of elation, or what is called a "runner's high." This natural drug produced by your body can become addictive in a very positive way.

People who develop the habit of regular, vigorous exercise find that it becomes easier and easier to do. They begin to look forward to the feeling of happiness they enjoy as the result of exercising aerobically.

*4. **Proper rest:*** This is very important. More than 60 percent of adults do not get enough sleep. They are suffering from what is called a "sleep deficit." They go to bed a little bit too late, sleep poorly, arise a little bit too early, and go through the day in a form of "fog." This phenomenon of not being sufficiently rested leads to poor performance, more mistakes, industrial accidents, car crashes, short tempers, personality problems, and many other difficulties.

If you are living and working a normal life, you require about eight hours of sleep each night. If you get only six or seven hours of sleep when you actually require eight, you begin to build up this sleep deficit. By Thursday or Friday, when you get up in the morning, the first thing you think of is how soon you can go back to sleep again that night. When you start thinking about going to sleep again at the moment that you arise, you know that you are not getting enough sleep.

In addition to eight hours of sleep per night, you need regular breaks from work, both weekends and vacations. When you take time off from work, you allow your mental and emotional batteries to recharge. After a two- or three-day weekend, when you go back to work, you will be fully rested and ready to perform at your best.

5. Proper attitude: This is perhaps the most important of all. The quality that is most predictive of health, happiness, and long life is "optimism." As you become more optimistic about yourself and your life, your health will also be better in every area.

People who are positive and optimistic usually have stronger immune systems, and as a result, they are seldom sick. They seldom get colds or flu. They bounce back quickly from hard work or fatigue. An optimistic person has a built-in "Teflon shield" against many of the diseases and ailments that affect the average person.

Get Your Weight Under Control

The biggest single problem with self-discipline that people have today is overeating and becoming ***overweight.*** More than 60 percent of Americans are officially overweight, and more than 30 percent are obese, which is defined as being more than 30 percent above their normal weight. There is no area in which self-discipline is more necessary than in getting your weight under control and then keeping it under control for the rest of your life.

You have heard it said that "diets don't work." What this really means is that when you starve yourself to lose weight, you will tend to put the weight back on almost as quickly as you lost it. There are many reasons for this.

Each person has a certain metabolic rate. This is the rate at which you burn energy. This metabolic rate is set over the course of your lifetime by the amount of food you eat relative to the amount of exercise you do to work it off.

In addition to your metabolic rate, you have what is called a "set point." This is where your weight is set, like a thermostat, and to which it returns no matter how much you take off as the result of crash dieting.

Change Your Set Point

To lose weight permanently, you must change your set point to a lower number. To achieve this, the first thing you do is to create a clear ***mental*** image of how you will look when you are at your ideal weight. Get a picture out of a magazine of someone who has the body you want to have, and then paste your photo where their face appears.

You then begin a gradual process of ***permanently*** changing the quality and quantity of what you eat, with no intention of ever going back. Be prepared to work on this permanent change for at least a *year*. Remember, if you are overweight, it has taken you many years to get to where you are today. Be prepared to invest a lot of time in getting back.

The Fatal Flaw in Dieting

Many people diet and lose weight with the idea that as soon as they have dropped a certain number of pounds, they can reward themselves by going out and having a fabulous meal or consuming unlimited desserts. In other words, they use the idea of filling up on food as the reward for losing weight in the first place. This approach is doomed to failure.

Instead, set up a reward system for yourself that does not include food. Decide instead to buy yourself new clothes that will fit you only at your ideal weight. Take yourself and your family on a vacation where you engage in fun activities. Make a bet with someone that you will take off the weight and keep it off for one year.

The Formula for Permanent Weight Loss

The key to perfect health can be summarized in five words: "Eat less and exercise more."

The only way that you can lose weight permanently is to burn off more calories than you consume. There is no other way. Moreover, you can do this only over an extended period of time, especially if you have allowed yourself to put on a lot of excess weight.

In my program, "Thinking Big," we teach the importance of avoiding the three white poisons: sugar, salt, and flour.

Get Rid of Sugar. To lose weight permanently and to enjoy high levels of health and energy, you should eliminate all simple sugars from your diet. Simple sugars are contained in candy, cake, pastries, desserts, soft drinks, canned fruits, sugar in your coffee, and all other forms of sugar that people consume in large quantities every day.

The fact is that you require ***no additional sugar*** to enjoy superb levels of physical health. Simply by eliminating all sugar and sugar products from your life, by going "cold turkey" on sugar, you will begin to lose as much as one pound per day.

Pass on the Salt. In addition, you should eliminate all additional salt from your diet. Although the average American gets sufficient salt in all the different foods he eats, he consumes an extra twenty pounds of salt each year by eating foods with high salt content and by then adding additional salt to meals.

When you consume excess salt, your body retains water in order to hold that salt in suspension. When you stop consuming excess salt and simultaneously drink eight glasses of water per day, your body releases all the excess fluid and you can actually experience weight drops of as much as four or five pounds in the first day.

Avoid White Flour Products. Finally, eliminate all white flour products from your diet. This means all breads, pastries, pastas, buns, rolls, and anything else made with white flour.

White flour is actually an "inert substance" from which all nutrients have been removed and then bleached out. When you see the words "enriched white bread," it means that the white flour, which is essentially a dead food material, has been fortified with artificial, chemical vitamins, almost all of which are then destroyed in the baking process. There is no food value in a white flour product.

A Simple Change of Diet

Not long ago, I got a letter from a thirty-two-year-old man in Florida. He told me that he had read my books and listened to my programs for years. He had achieved a higher level of financial and career success than he ever imagined possible. But he was still carrying an extra twenty pounds of weight that he could not get rid of, no matter what he did.

Then one day, he listened to "Thinking Big," and he heard my comments on the three white poisons. Fortunately, he was both disciplined and determined. He used his willpower to slam the brakes on these three foods and discontinue them completely.

He said that what happened next was nothing short of miraculous. Within six months, he had dropped twenty-two pounds. When he wrote to me, he had kept them off for two years. He said that he looked different, felt different, was more attractive to women, and had higher levels of self-confidence and self-esteem. His whole life had improved since he dropped the excess weight.

Live to Be One Hundred

Your goal in life should be to enjoy the highest levels of health and energy possible. This requires that you eat the right foods and *fewer* of them. It requires that you get regular exercise and move every joint of your body every single day.

To enjoy superb physical health, you must get lots of rest and recreation. Above all, you must maintain a positive mental attitude in which you look for the good in every situation and remain determined to be a completely positive person.

In each of these areas, the exertion of self-discipline and willpower will give you payoffs that are far beyond the effort that you put in. By practicing self-discipline in your health habits, you can live longer and better than you ever imagined possible. Chapter 17 provides even more ideas, specifically focused on exercise and becoming physically fit.

Action Exercises:

1. Idealize with regard to your health: If you could wave a magic wand and make your health *perfect* in every way, how would it be different from today?
2. Resolve to make the rest of your life the *best* of your life. What is the first thing you should change or do?
3. Get a complete medical examination and ask your doctor for advice on how to enjoy superb levels of physical health. Then *follow* that advice.

4. Determine your ideal weight and set it as a goal. Use the goal-setting process you learned in Chapter 4 to make a plan to achieve it and keep it there for life.
5. Use mindstorming (described in Chapter 4) and write out a list of at least twenty answers to the question, "What can I do every day to enjoy superb levels of health and energy?"
6. Review the health habits and research discussed in this chapter and give yourself a grade ranging from one to ten on how well you are practicing them.
7. Decide on ***one*** specific action that you are going to take immediately to ensure that you live to be age eighty, ninety, and beyond.

Chapter 17

Self-Discipline and Physical Fitness

"Mental toughness is many things and rather difficult to explain. Its qualities are sacrifice and self denial. Also, and most importantly, it is combined with a perfectly disciplined will that refuses to give in. It is a state of mind that you could call character in action."

—VINCE LOMBARDI

For you to achieve and maintain high levels of physical fitness requires a lifetime of self-discipline and willpower. The good news is that physical fitness is its own reward. Not only do you feel good while you are exercising, but you feel wonderful about yourself the rest of the time.

If your goal is to live a long, healthy, happy life and be fit and trim physically, there is no substitute for regular exercise. Fortunately, you do not have to train for the Olympics or a triathlon to enjoy superb levels of physical well-being. By building exercise and physical training into your daily routine you can achieve physical fitness just by making a few small modifications to your lifestyle.

• • •

Listen to the Experts

Physical fitness specialists generally agree that you need to exercise 200–300 minutes per week to enjoy the maximum levels of physical well-being that are possible for you. This means that you need to exercise between thirty and sixty minutes, five to seven times each week.

At the low end, if you simply went for a thirty-minute walk each morning before you started off for work or each evening when you got home from work as well as each weekend day, you would be one of the healthiest people in our society.

If you increase your exercise level to sixty minutes each time, five times per week, you will be in the top 1 or 2 percent of physically fit people in the world today.

Get Started First Thing

The best time to exercise is first thing in the morning. People who get up each morning and exercise for thirty to sixty minutes are much more likely to make exercise a permanent part of their daily routine.

On the other hand, people who put off exercising until later in the day, until after work, almost invariably find that they are too tired or have too many other things to do.

They procrastinate on exercising until another day, which often never comes.

It takes tremendous discipline to get into and follow a regular exercise routine. But it is easier if you can discipline yourself to get up in the morning and start exercising immediately.

Trick Yourself

Many people, including myself, trick themselves into exercising in the morning by putting their exercise clothes right next to the bed so that they trip over them when they get up. Before they are even awake, they find themselves pulling on their exercise clothes and running shoes and starting off around the block. Before they even know what has happened, they are halfway into their exercise routine, their heart rate is up, their lungs are puffing away, and they are feeling good about themselves.

Whenever people come back from a morning run or any other form of morning exercise, they are always happy and smiling. This is because of the "exercise effect" that kicks in after twenty-five or thirty minutes. Their brains release endorphins and they feel exhilarated.

Increase Your Intelligence

People who engage in aerobic exercise first thing in the morning have been shown to be brighter, more creative, and more intelligent throughout the day. They actually score ***higher*** on intelligence tests, and they seem to come up with more ideas to help them do their work better during the course of the day.

The reason for this is obvious. When you engage in aerobic exercise first thing in the morning, you drive hyperoxygenated blood into your cerebral cortex, the part of your brain that you use for thinking, analyzing, and decision making. This makes you wide-awake and alert from first thing in the morning and then for several hours afterward.

When you exercise as soon as you get up, you kick your metabolic rate into a higher gear. As a result, your body continues to burn calories all day long. You continue to lose weight for several hours after exercising.

When you exercise first thing in the morning or anytime during the day, you become hungry. However, because you are working out your body in such a healthy way, you will have a natural appetite for healthy foods. You will have little or no desire for sweet foods or desserts.

Make Exercise a Part of Your Lifestyle

One of the best things you can do to achieve and maintain high levels of physical fitness is to join a gym or a health club and attend regular exercise classes. You can even pay a little more and get yourself a personal trainer who puts you through an exercise regimen three or more times each week.

You are much more likely to discipline yourself to start and maintain a fitness routine if you have someone who is expecting you to be at a class or monitoring you on a regular basis to make sure that you follow the exercise program to which you committed.

Many people today are hiring personal trainers. Either a personal trainer can come to your home or place of work or you can go to a gym that has personal trainers on staff who will work with you on the specific equipment you want to use.

People who use personal trainers are almost universally delighted with the results. They find that being accountable to a trainer exerts a positive influence on them, causing them to eat less so they have less weight to burn off and to work harder when they exercise so that they can earn the approval of the trainer.

Join an Organized Sport

Organized sports are a wonderful way to achieve and maintain high levels of physical fitness. They are far more demanding in terms of time and schedule, but the payoff is often extraordinary.

If you are a member of a sports league—whether that be baseball, tennis, football, soccer, racquetball, or anything else—and you have a coach or trainer that you work with on a regular basis, you tend to be more focused and disciplined. You will exercise more often and more vigorously, and you will be fitter and trimmer than most other people.

Develop New and Better Habits

Unfortunately, physical fitness and sports training require such high levels of ***discipline***, and few people are capable of starting and continuing this kind of exercise regimen. For better or worse, whatever you do repeatedly becomes a habit, and many people get out of the habit of regular exercise and never go back.

Fortunately, it is never too late. At any time, you can decide that you are going to enjoy high levels of physical fitness. You can make a decision, ***right now,*** to start a physical fitness routine of some kind and then set it as a personal test or challenge to see if you have the willpower and ***discipline*** to follow through on your resolution.

You Can Start Today

Some years ago, there was a sixty-eight-year-old woman living in a senior citizens' home who had never given much thought to physical exercise. She had worked hard, raised her family, become a grandmother, and was now living comfortably in a senior citizens' residence.

One day, she saw a television special on jogging. During this special, they interviewed a couple of people in their fifties and sixties who were running marathons. Some of them had started running later in life.

This sixty-eight-year-old woman decided that she wanted to run a marathon as well. She drove down to a nearby store and bought the proper shoes for walking and running. That day, she began her exercise regimen by walking around the neighborhood where she lived. Over the next few weeks, she walked ever-greater distances. She bought books and sought advice on how to exercise and train her legs for running.

Build Up Gradually

After two months, she began jogging a little as part of her walking routine. After six months, she began running as part of her walking and jogging routine. By the end of the first year, she had run in a mini-marathon in her local community.

By the time she was seventy-five, she had completed ten 26.4-mile marathons and two fifty-mile cross-country marathons. And the most remarkable thing was that she had never run before the age of sixty-eight.

So what's ***your*** excuse? If this sixty-eight-year-old woman could start exercising so late in life, why can't ***you***?

One of the greatest guarantors that you will live a long, happy life, being bright, alert, and full of energy, is that you begin a regular physical training program, four or five days per week, and continue it for the rest of your life.

When you exert your self-discipline and willpower to achieve a high level of physical fitness and then maintain it year after year, you will feel terrific about yourself.

In the next chapter, you learn how self-discipline in ***marriage*** can have a wonderful effect in assuring a long life of happiness and fulfillment with another person.

Action Exercises:

1. Today is the day! Make a decision that you are going to achieve the best physical condition of your life in the months ahead, and then take action immediately.
2. Get a complete medical examination so that you know your condition and limits before you begin.
3. Start walking thirty minutes each day, preferably first thing in the morning or, if not in the morning, right after work.
4. Join a gym or health club, pay for a *year*, and make an appointment with yourself to work out five times a week, sixty minutes each time.

5. Hire a personal trainer and have him/her guide you through an exercise program that includes aerobics, strength, and flexibility exercises each week.
6. Invest in a treadmill, a LifeCycle, or an elliptical machine and put it in front of your television so you can exercise as part of your home and family life.
7. Start gradually and work up slowly, resolving to exercise for several weeks before you notice a major difference. Be patient, persistent, and determined.

Chapter 18

Self-Discipline and Marriage

"It is better to control yourself than to win a thousand battles. Then the victory is yours. It cannot be taken from you, not by angels or demons, heaven or hell."

—BUDDHA

Your ability to enter into a long-term, loving relationship is an important measure of your character and personality.

Men and women are born to be two halves that make up one whole. They have different qualities and characteristics that, when properly combined, achieve completion and the balance and harmony that nature demands.

The foundational qualities for marriage and loving relationships are trust and respect. Men and women can have many disagreements over the course of their married life together, but as long as the trust and respect between them endure, the marriage can go on indefinitely. If ever one or the other party can no longer trust the other or no longer respects the other, the relationship is finished.

Many marriages end in divorce and many divorced people have multiple marriages, each of which ends in failure. Yet some people get married once and stay married contentedly for the rest of their lives. Why is this?

The Key to a Happy Marriage

Perhaps the most important reason for a happy marriage is ***compatibility***. The two people are ideally balanced with each other, with each one possessing complementary qualities and characteristics that combine comfortably to form a perfect balance.

People often say that "opposites attract." This is a misunderstanding. Opposites attract in only one area, and that is ***temperament***. You will always be most compatible with a person who has an opposite or counterbalancing temperament to your own.

For example, if you are outgoing and extroverted, you will be most compatible with a person who is more reserved and self-contained. If you are voluble and expressive, you will be most compatible with a person who is relaxed and a good listener. Nature demands a balance in temperament for two people to be compatible and happy together.

Birds of a Feather

In all other areas, especially in the area of ***values***, it is similarities that attract. Birds of a feather do flock together. You will always be attracted to people and most compatible with those who have the greatest number of fundamental values in common with yourself.

All of love, of any kind, is a response to ***value***. We love what we most value, both in ourselves and others. When a couple is truly happy together, they seem to have very much the same values regarding family, money, ethics, work, children, politics, religion, and people.

People will often point out that there are happy couples who vote for different parties or come from different religious backgrounds. But the critical issue in balance and harmony revolves around the ***intensity*** with which a person values something. This intensity determines if a person is absolute and unbending or relaxed and flexible in his or her adherence to a particular belief about a particular part of life.

People can love and live together happily for many years even though they support different political parties, as long as political belief is not so important to either of them that it takes precedence over more important elements of their relationship such as children, family, and values.

Love Is Our Greatest Need in Life

It is said that "everything we do in life is either to get love, or to compensate for a lack of love." Psychologists generally agree that the root cause of personality problems in adult life can be traced back to "love withheld" in infancy and childhood.

People need love like roses need rain. Without sufficient love and acceptance, individuals exhibit all kinds of personality and physical problems. It is only possible to be happy when your needs for love are completely fulfilled.

A happy marriage requires tremendous self-discipline and self-control. Love requires self-denial and sacrifice. When you are truly in love with another person, that person's happiness and well-being become more important than your own. You are willing to pay whatever price and make whatever sacrifice in order to ensure the well-being of the person you love.

In the Christian Bible, in a letter to the Corinthians, the apostle Paul says, "Love suffereth long, and is kind; love envieth not; love avengeth not itself, is not puffed up.

"Love doth not behave itself unseemly, seeketh not his own, is not easily provoked, thinketh no evil;

"Love rejoices not in iniquity, but rejoices in the truth;

"Love beareth all things, believeth all things, hopeth all things, endureth all things. Love never fails."

Different Strokes Require Tolerance and Understanding

Each person is an individual, with unique and special characteristics that make him or her different from all other people. Each person has different ideas, tastes, desires, hopes, dreams, and expectations. Each person has had different experiences and developed different ways of seeing and dealing with the world around him or her.

When you come together with another person in a loving relationship, no matter how close you feel to each other and no matter how compatible you may be in many ways, you will still have areas of disagreement, dissatisfaction, and discontent. This is normal and natural and something to be worked through by practicing self-discipline and self-control whenever these differences occur.

Self-discipline in a relationship requires that you be completely honest and open, that you be yourself and never try to be someone or something else. Self-discipline and honesty require that you state clearly what you are thinking and feeling, without anger or irritation, and that you listen calmly and patiently to the feelings, thoughts, and opinions of the other person.

Male-Female Communication Styles

Men and women are different in many ways. According to MRI scans, when men communicate, they use only two centers of their brains. When women communicate, they use seven centers of their brains. It is as though men have two headlights with which to communicate, whereas a woman's brain is like a fully lit Christmas tree.

Men can process only ***one*** sensory input at a time, whereas women can process multiple sensory inputs. When a man is watching television, he does not see or hear anything else, including words spoken to him from the side or behind. He becomes totally fixated on the visual images and words on the screen.

When a man is driving a car, he has to turn down the radio to read the map. He has to turn down the television or radio to answer the telephone. He cannot read and listen or watch at the same time. Men can do many things extremely well, but they can do only one thing at a time. Men tend to be very focused.

Women, on the other hand, can talk, make dinner, watch television, read the day's mail, and talk to her children or husband all at once. They are multidimensional and can process several inputs simultaneously. They can talk and listen at the same time and be aware of what other people around them are doing and saying.

Women are relationship experts. They are very sensitive to other people. When a man and a woman attend a social gathering, within ten minutes, the woman will have done an analysis and assessment of the situation of each of the other people in the room. In contrast, the man accompanying the woman will have noticed little or nothing. This is because men are simple and straightforward in their thinking, whereas women are complex, aware of small details, and extremely sensitive to the dynamics and nuances of the relationships of the people around them.

A man can call his wife on the phone and say, "Hello." Although she has only heard one word, she will immediately ask, "What's wrong?" She can pick up a wealth of meaning and emotion from a single word on the phone or a single glance or look when he walks in the door.

• • •

Relationship-Building Takes Effort

Because of the many differences between men and women, it takes tremendous discipline to build and maintain a long-term, loving, and happy relationship.

Perhaps the most important area of mutual compatibility has to do with the discipline of ***listening***. It is only when two people take the time to listen closely and carefully to each other when they speak that the lines of communications stay open, and this is when love and harmony continue in the relationship.

There are four simple disciplines of effective listening. They are mostly of importance to men, who are notoriously poor listeners, especially with the women in their lives. This is not because they are not interested. It is simply because their minds are focused on something else and they are easily distracted.

The Disciplines of Listening

Listen Attentively. The first discipline is to listen ***attentively***, without interrupting. Listen as though the other person is about to reveal a great secret or the winning lottery number and you will hear it only once.

When she wants to talk to you, if you are a man, put aside all possible distractions. Turn off the television or radio. Put down the newspaper or mail. Face her directly, lean slightly forward, and concentrate single-mindedly on what she is saying.

The book ***His Needs, Her Needs*** points out that the most important need that a woman has from a man is

affection. Affection is expressed by paying total attention to her when she speaks. Since you always pay attention to what you most value, when you pay close attention to another person while she speaks, you tell that person that she is of great value to you. This satisfies the deepest subconscious needs of a woman—to feel valuable, important, and respected.

Pause before Replying. The second discipline of listening is to pause before replying. Take a few seconds to carefully consider what he or she has said. When you pause, you avoid the risk of interrupting the other person if she is just reformulating her thoughts. You tell her that you value what she said and that you are giving her words careful consideration.

Another advantage of pausing, of allowing a silence in the conversation, is that it enables you to hear not only what was said, but also what was ***not*** said or what was said between the lines. The actual message soaks into a deeper level of your mind, enabling you to understand better and to therefore respond with greater awareness and sensitivity.

Ask for Clarification. The third discipline of effective listening is to question for clarification. Never assume that you automatically know what the other person is thinking or feeling. Instead, if you are at all unclear, simply ask, "How do you mean?" or "How do you mean, exactly?"

It is when you ask questions and seek clarity and meaning that you demonstrate to the other person that you really care about what he or she is saying, and that you are genuinely interested in understanding how he or she thinks and feels.

Feed It Back. The fourth discipline of effective listening is for you to feed back what the other person has said, and ***paraphrase*** it in your own words. This is the "acid test" of listening. This is where you demonstrate to the other person that you were genuinely paying attention. It is only when you can repeat back what the other person has just said, in your own words, that you prove to him or her that you were really listening.

Most problems in relationships arise because of poor communication. The couple does not talk together often enough or one or the other does not listen attentively when the other wants to speak.

Each person has an emotional need to ***talk*** a certain amount with his or her spouse. Each person also has an emotional need to ***listen*** a certain amount. The most compatible couples are those in whom the desire to talk and listen are in balance with each other. There is an easy ebb and flow of conversation, punctuated with comfortable silences. Each person gets a chance to fulfill his or her need for both talking and listening, and both parties are content.

Total Commitment Is Essential

Love and marriage require total commitment on the part of both people. It takes tremendous discipline to go "all in" in a relationship. What's more, this is also tremendously liberating. It is only when you are totally committed to a relationship with a single person that you are completely free to turn your attention toward fulfilling your potential in the other aspects of your life.

One of the most important disciplines in a marriage or relationship is that of ***faithfulness***. Because we live in a highly sexualized society, there are temptations and provocations around us all the time and virtually everywhere we go. It often takes considerable self-discipline and self-control to be completely loyal to your spouse throughout your married life.

There are two ways to help you avoid the regular temptations that can damage or even destroy the most loving of relationships.

First, make a decision, in advance, that you will never, never be unfaithful to your spouse. Like drawing a line in the sand, make the decision in advance that no matter what happens, you will not stray for any reason.

Second, discipline yourself to stay out of harm's way. Refuse to go anywhere or do anything where temptation may exist. Except when essential for business purposes, avoid having lunch, drinks, or dinner alone with a member of the opposite sex. Remember, there is safety in crowds.

Continually imagine, everywhere you go and in everything you do, that your spouse is standing right next to you, watching and listening to what you say and do. Imagine that anything and everything you do, no matter where you are, is going to be reported back to your spouse within twenty-four hours. Use your discipline and willpower to build and maintain a reputation for being a completely honest and faithful spouse.

Be Willing to Change

Every marriage is a "work in progress." As time passes, the nature of your marriage will change, usually in positive and constructive ways.

To keep your relationship happy, harmonious, and growing, you must be willing to change in response to changing circumstances, especially having children and watching them grow up. You need to be prepared to change with age, new jobs and careers, physical moves from one part of the country to another, changes in financial circumstances, and changes in health. Flexibility is absolutely essential to a long, happy marriage.

There are only ***four*** ways that you can change your life. First, you can do ***more*** of some things. Second, you can do ***less*** of other things. Third, you can ***start*** something that you have never done before. And fourth, you can ***stop*** certain things altogether. Whenever you are experiencing resistance or frustration or you are confronted with the need for change, ask yourself, "Is there anything that I need to do more of, less of, start, or stop doing?"

The Four Questions You Should Ask

On a regular basis, you should sit down with your spouse and later with your children to have the courage to ask them these four questions:

1. Is there anything that I am doing that you would like me to do more of?
2. Is there anything that I am doing that you would like me to do less of?
3. Is there anything that you would like me to start doing that I am not doing today?
4. Is there anything that I am doing that you would like me to stop doing altogether?

When you have the courage and discipline to ask these questions of your spouse and your children on a regular basis, you will be amazed at the quality and depth of the answers you receive. You will get continual guidance on how you can modify and adjust your behaviors to maintain higher levels of harmony, happiness, and love with your spouse and the other members of your family.

Your Spouse Should Be Your Best Friend

Love and marriage are perhaps the most important elements of a happy, fulfilling life. They require a lifelong exercise of self-discipline and willpower to create and maintain harmony. They require that you be open, honest, and candid at all times.

Most of all, a happy, a loving marriage requires that you see your spouse as your ***best friend***. There should be no one in the world who you would rather spend time with more than him or her. There should be no one with whom you are more open and honest than with him or her. When you see your spouse as your best friend and treat him or her as such, you can create a loving relationship that lasts all the days of your lives.

As Emmet Fox, a spiritual writer and teacher, wrote,

> Love is by far the most important thing of all. It casts out fear. It is the fulfilling of the law. It covers a multitude of sins. Love is absolutely invincible.
>
> There is no difficulty that enough love will not cure; no disease that enough love will not heal; no door that enough love will not open; no gulf that enough love will not bridge; no wall that enough love will not throw down; no sin that enough love will not redeem.
>
> It makes no difference how deeply seated may be the trouble, how hopeless the outlook, how muddled the tangle, how great the mistake; a sufficient realization of love will dissolve it all.
>
> If only you could love enough you would be the happiest and most powerful being in the world.

In the next chapter, you will learn specifically why self-discipline is so important when raising happy, healthy, and self-confident ***children***.

Action Exercises:

1. What is the most important single action you could take, right now, to increase the love and harmony in your marriage or relationship?
2. What disciplines or practices could you develop that would improve the quality of your marriage for the other person?
3. Identify one behavior you could engage in that would improve your communications in your marriage.
4. Sit down with your spouse and ask him/her for ideas for things that you should do more of, less of, start, or stop doing.

5. Identify the two qualities that you most admire in your partner.
6. Identify the areas in which you and your partner are the most compatible.
7. Identify the most important values that you and your partner share.

Chapter 19

Self-Discipline and Children

"Right discipline exists, not in external compulsion, but in habits of mind which lead spontaneously to desirable rather than undesirable activities."
—BERTRAND RUSSELL

You can calculate the value or importance of something you do by measuring the possible ***consequences*** of doing or not doing it. Something that is important is something that has significant potential consequences, like jumping out of the path of a speeding car. Bringing children into the world has consequences that can go on for eighty years (which is the average life expectancy of a person today) and beyond, into the lives of your grandchildren and great grandchildren. This is why becoming a parent is one of the most important things you will ever do.

As an adult, you are still affected today by things that your grandparents did or didn't do to or for your parents. The way you treat your children is strongly influenced by the way your parents treated you. It has consequences that cascade down the generations, and it has an enormous influence on their lifelong happiness and well-being.

Your Greatest Responsibility

When you have a child, a high level of self-discipline is essential in order to fulfill your commitment and deliver on your responsibility. The day your first child is born, you have taken on a minimum twenty-year commitment to do everything possible to raise your child as a happy, healthy, and self-confident adult.

At every stage of your child's life, your words, actions, nonactions, and behaviors are shaping and influencing that child and determining how he or she will turn out as an adult.

The greatest need that a child has is for an unbroken flow of ***unconditional*** love and acceptance from his or her parents. Children need love almost as much as they need oxygen. The amount of love that a child receives, especially in his or her formative years, is the critical determinant of how healthy and happy he or she becomes as an adult.

How Children Spell "Love"

How does a child spell "love"? T-I-M-E. Children determine how valuable and important they are and develop their self-esteem and self-worth by measuring the amount of time that the most important people in their lives spend with them when they are young. There is no substitute for time, and once gone, you cannot make it up. Perhaps the greatest regret reported by parents is that "I didn't spend enough time with my child when he or she was young."

When you become a parent, you must ***discipline*** yourself and organize your life so you can spend ample time with your child throughout his or her growing years. You must discipline yourself to cut back, reduce, downsize, and eliminate other activities that prevent you from being an excellent parent.

A Wake-up Call

Some years ago, a good friend of mine got married. He was an avid golfer, and he regularly played golf five times a week, often flying south in the winter for golf vacations when his local golf courses were covered with snow.

Within four years of marrying, he and his wife had four children. Nonetheless, he still tried to play golf several times a week, taking time off from his business during the week and playing on weekends.

Finally, his wife confronted him and told him that he was not spending enough time with his young children. His golf was taking up too many hours that would be better spent at home with her and with the children, especially during their most vulnerable and sensitive years.

He suddenly realized that his life had changed. The things that he could do when he was single were no longer possible when he had young children. Being highly responsible and self-disciplined, he immediately cut back his golf to once per week and rechanneled his time and energy into his family. He told me later that it made an extraordinary difference to his marriage and to his relationships with his young children.

Setting New Priorities

When you get married, your life goes though a major shift. Your lifestyle changes, and many of your common activities lose their importance and urgency.

When your first child is born, your life shifts again. It often feels as if the first stage of your life—your youth—has dropped off, like the first stage of a rocket, and you are now on a different trajectory in life. In fact, it is not uncommon for couples to change their lives completely when their first child is born. They cut back or discontinue many of their previous social activities. They stop dining and drinking with friends, and they stop going out socially on the weekends.

They begin to build a different life together around their home and children. The children become the focus of their time and attention. The children become the primary subject of their conversations.

Responsible parents approach childrearing as the most important part of their lives. They plan and organize their time and activities so they can fulfill this responsibility at a high level.

Long-Term Thinking

Children force you to think long-term. When you realize that everything that you do or fail to do with your children in their formative years will have a lasting impact for generations to come, you become far more thoughtful and sensitive to the things you say and the way you treat them.

When you are young and single, you can "let it all hang out." You can blow up, get angry, express your feelings freely, and "be your own person." But when you have a child, you need to impose a higher level of discipline and self-control on yourself.

Children are hypersensitive to the influence of their parents during their formative years. They see and experience each word and reaction of their parents, and they incorporate those words and actions into their world view and self-image.

In almost every case, when you see a dysfunctional adult, you can trace it back to dysfunctional parenting. When that dysfunctional adult was a child, their parents did or said things to them that hurt them, confused them, scared them, and created within them feelings of insecurity, anger, and inferiority.

The Greatest Gift Is Love

The greatest gift you can give children is to let them know that you love them 100 percent of the time and that your love for them never changes, no matter what happens.

There is no greater blessing for children than to know with complete confidence that the most important people in their life—their parents—love them completely and accept them totally, no matter what they do or what mistakes they make.

Children are not ***little adults***. They do not have the ability to make good judgments about the right or wrong things to do. It takes them many years of trial and error and sometimes bitter experience to develop the wisdom and judgment that enable them to make good decisions for themselves and their futures.

The kindest way to treat your children when they make mistakes is to behave with calmness and compassion and to help them learn the lessons contained in the problem or difficulty.

Discipline Versus Development

Many parents think that their job is to discipline their children by punishing them when they make a mistake. Back in the 1930s, when my parents were growing up, it was generally taught that the job of the parent was to "break the will of the child." This philosophy led to a generation of broken children whose parents felt that it was their duty to mold them and shape them into little people that their parents found to be acceptable.

But the fact is that each child is unique and different from all other people in the world. Each child comes into this world with his or her unique temperament, personality, and natural leanings toward different interests and activities.

Parents are often amazed to see that each of their children is very different from each other child, even though they come from the same parents and grow up in the same household. In my experience, each child "marches to the beat of a different drummer."

No matter what you do to or for them, they have their own special destiny. They are going to grow up with a particular personality, and they will be attracted to particular people and activities. Your main job is to create an environment in which they feel safe and confident enough to follow their inner promptings and personal inclinations.

Question Your Beliefs

A philosopher once said, "Before I had children, I had four philosophies about raising children. Now, I have four children, and no philosophies."

Each child is different from any other child and from any other person. When raising your children, be prepared to question your most cherished beliefs about what they "should" or "should not" do, say, or be. Above all, be prepared to admit that you could be ***wrong***, because you are going to make more mistakes than you can imagine.

Perhaps the most important responsibility you have as a parent is to instill ***values*** in your children, especially the value of self-discipline. One of the most common desires that parents have for their children is to raise them with a sense of self-responsibility and self-control. Parents want their children to be self-disciplined and to practice self-mastery and self-denial, or the ability to delay gratification.

Set a Good Example

Albert Schweitzer once wrote, "You must teach men at the school of example, for they will learn at no other."

The most powerful influence you have on your children is the example that you set for them all the time that they are growing up. Your children are always watching you out of the corners of their eyes or from another room. They take everything in. They measure and analyze your behaviors, especially when you are ***under stress***. By watching the way you behave, especially when you are angry or upset or when they have made a mistake, they develop a clear picture for themselves of how adults are supposed to behave in the world.

Your example sets the standard that they consider to be the normal way that adults act in various circumstances, especially when under stress. Your children, if they admire and respect your example, will strive ***to emulate you*** while they are growing up and then continuing on for the rest of their lives.

Perhaps the best question you can ask yourself, over and over, is, "What kind of a family would my family be if everyone in it were just like me?"

Be a Role Model

When you practice self-discipline and self-control, especially when you feel angry or upset, your children absorb the lesson. Later, when they are angry or upset, ***they*** will practice self-discipline and self-control as well.

In a recent study, researchers concluded that children form their idea of the world by watching how their ***mother*** deals with the ups and downs of daily life. If their mother seems calm, relaxed, and in control, children assume that this is a logical and rational world so they are much more likely to practice calmness and self-control themselves.

If their mother seems to be frustrated, angry, or overwhelmed by too much to do and too little time, children absorb the world view that life is confused and stressful.

Building Character

The most important job you have as a parent is to instill values and to build ***character*** in your children. You do this by teaching them what values are important, especially those of integrity and truth telling. You set yourself up as a role model and demonstrate the values you want your children to have in every situation where those values are called for.

Because the core value of character is ***integrity***, the most important value that you instill in your children is ***truthfulness***. Much to the shock of most parents, children lie. When they are growing up, they don't tell the truth. They tell both little and big lies. Often, this comes as a surprise to parents who feel that somehow they must have failed their children in some way.

But don't worry: Lying is a normal and natural part of childhood. It is a form of communication that children are trying out on you to see if it works. If children find that telling lies is an effective way to get the things they want quickly and easily, they will lie on a regular basis.

For example, I once asked my son Michael a question, and he gave me an answer that I knew was completely untrue. I asked him, "Michael, why did you say that? You know that that's a barefaced lie!" Michael, who was ten years old at the time, answered candidly, "Well, I just thought I'd give it a try."

Children will give lying a try to see if it works. If it doesn't, they will try something else, and that something else is usually telling the truth.

Always Tell the Truth

One day, my wife and I read a question in a book on child raising, which said, "If your children lie to you, who has made them afraid to tell the truth?"

That was a real eye-opener for us. We immediately sat down with our children and told them, "From now on, always tell the truth. We promise you that you will never get into trouble for telling the truth. If you tell a lie, we will be upset and you will be punished. But if you tell the truth, you will always be okay with us."

From that day onward, with few exceptions, our children "tried us out" with the truth. Over time, they got into a habit of telling the truth, no matter what it was. And we kept our promise. We never punished our children for telling the truth.

One day, as we were sitting around the family dinner table, one of our children was talking about his friend who had told him to lie to us about something he was planning to do.

My son said, "I told him that I never lie to my parents."

His friend said, "Everyone lies to their parents."

My son repeated, "I never lie to my parents, because I don't have to. I can always tell them the truth and everything will be okay."

Our three children listened to this, and they all agreed. They told us that this was a great family because they never had to lie to their parents.

The Foundation of Self-Confidence

When children tell the truth, they grow up straight and strong, with high self-esteem and high levels of self-confidence. They have higher levels of self-respect and personal pride. They look you straight in the eye and tell you exactly what they are thinking and feeling. They are very different from children who must continually lie or shade the truth in order to get things past their parents.

In raising your children, there will be countless times when they will do or say something which you disapprove of or which makes you angry. During these times you must discipline yourself to think before you act, or react, controlling yourself and your temper. You must remind yourself that what you do in a moment of stress is registered and recorded by your child and can have an effect on him or her for an indefinite period into the future.

Children learn values by teaching and example, given to them repeatedly while they're growing up. When you teach them values and personally practice the values of love—especially for your spouse—compassion for those who are less fortunate, generosity with those who need it, patience when it is required, tolerance for different viewpoints, courage in the face of difficulties, and perseverance in the face of setbacks, your children will adopt these behaviors as norms. They will see them as the appropriate way to respond to these kinds of situations as they grow up.

The Power of Forgiveness

One of the most important of all values that you teach your children is ***forgiveness***. The inability to forgive lies at the root of most negative emotions. When you practice forgiveness, when you freely let things go, your children grow up with the ability to forgive as well. This saves them from years of unhappiness as the result of someone hurting them in some way, which will always happen.

My parents were adamant and inflexible. They had low self-esteem as the result of difficult Depression-era childhoods. As a result, once they had taken a position on any subject, however wrong, they could never back down and admit that they were wrong.

I resolved that when I had children, I would do exactly the opposite. From the time my daughter Christina was a little girl, if I shouted at her for any reason, I would always go to her and apologize. I would say, "I should not have shouted at you. I was wrong. Will you forgive me?"

When you raise children, they will make countless mistakes while they are growing up. Sometimes you will overreact. Unless you are a saint, this is almost impossible for you not to do. However, whenever you make a mistake with your child, you should have the courage and compassion to realize that destructive criticism from a parent is extremely painful to a child. Go and take it back. Apologize and ask your child for forgiveness. Even if the child has misbehaved, this does not justify reacting in a negative and hurtful way toward your child. Just say, "I apologize. Will you forgive me?"

And they always will. The minute you apologize and ask your children to forgive you for anything that you may have done to hurt them, you liberate them from feelings of negativity or inferiority. By taking it back, you allow them to be happy and confident once more.

Teaching Your Children Is Never Ending

Developing proper values and teaching proper conduct to your children is a lifelong job. You cannot give a single lecture on truthfulness and compassion and then forget about it. You must repeat the lesson by discussion and example over and over, year after year, all the time while your children are with you.

In a letter to Miss Manners, a parent asked, "How long does it take to teach my children table manners? No matter what I say, it seems that my children still eat in an unmannered and disorganized way." Miss Manners responded by saying, "Be patient. It takes about fifteen years of continual repetition to teach your children table manners. And even then, there are no guarantees that your instruction will be successful."

Be Their Role Model

Of course, if you want your children to behave in a certain way, you must model that method of behavior continually, year after year. If you want your children to dress properly, ***you*** must dress properly. If you want your children to groom themselves properly, ***you*** must groom yourself properly as well. If you want your children to be organized and efficient, ***you*** must show them the way by being organized and efficient yourself.

Remember each day that your children are going to behave the way that you behave for the rest of their lives. When you think like this, it forces you to practice higher levels of self-discipline and self-control, knowing that the consequences of your behaviors are going to affect your children's chances in life many years from now.

The discipline of raising children so that they grow up with high self-esteem, being positive and confident in themselves and their own value, is one of the most important things you ever do. The results of your childrearing will last you all the years of your life.

Action Exercises:

1. What two qualities would you like your children to identify with you by observing your behavior?
2. What two qualities would you like most to instill in your children, and how could you achieve this?
3. If you were an excellent role model for your children, how would your behaviors be different, starting today?

4. What mistakes have your children made that you should forgive and forget about, starting immediately?
5. What actions are you going to take immediately to spend more time with your children?
6. What actions could you take to instill the quality of truthfulness in your children?
7. How could you encourage and reward your children so that they practice greater self-discipline, self-control, and self-mastery?

Chapter 20

Self-Discipline and Friendship

"Everything you want in life
has a price connected to it. There is a price to pay
if you want to make things better, a price to pay
for leaving things as they are, a price for everything."
—Harry Browne

Fully 85 percent of your happiness will come from happy relationships with other people. Unfortunately, fully 85 percent of your problems and unhappiness will be associated with other people as well. Chapters 18 and 19 offered some ideas on how to have a happier marriage and raise happier children, but in addition to your family, of course, your friendships are also important to your well-being.

It therefore behooves you to become absolutely excellent at human relations. Fortunately, this is a learnable skill. You can become one of the most popular people in your work and social circle by simply engaging in the behaviors that ***other*** popular people practice on a regular basis.

Aristotle wrote that man is a social animal. This means that we define ourselves in terms of our relationships with other people. Our destinies are determined by our interactions with others and theirs with us. We learn who we are and know about ourselves only through interacting with other people.

The Core of Personality

Psychologists tell us that everything we do is either to build our self-esteem or to protect it from being torn down by other people. Each person is hypersensitive about his or her own sense of personal value and importance.

Your self-esteem—how you feel about yourself, how much you like yourself—is largely determined by your self-image, or the way you see and think about yourself. Your self-image is made up of three parts, like the three wedges of a pie, each touching the others:

1. First, your self-image is made up of ***the way you see yourself.*** This largely determines the way you walk, talk, behave, and interact with others.
2. The second part of your self-image is the way you ***think*** others see you. If you think other people like, respect, and admire you, you see yourself in a positive way and you enjoy higher feelings of self-esteem and self-importance.
3. The third part of your self-image is the way people ***actually*** do see you and treat you. If you think you are well liked and popular and some-

one treats you in a rude or disrespectful way, it can be a shock to your self-image and lower your self-esteem. On the other hand, if you see yourself as an average person, and the people you meet treat you as though you are a valuable and important person, you can experience a ***positive*** shock to your self-image that causes you to like and value yourself even more.

The Key to Happiness

You are truly happy only when you feel that all three parts of your self-image coincide. You are happy only when you feel that the way you see yourself, the way you think others see you, and the way they actually see you all seem to be consistent in a particular situation.

In life, you seek out friendships and relationships with people who make you feel comfortable with the way you see yourself and think about yourself. When you are with people who treat you as if you are valuable and important, you enjoy higher levels of self-esteem. You like and respect yourself more. You feel happy in their presence.

For example, in school you always did better and got better grades when you felt that the teacher liked you and cared about you. At work, perhaps the greatest motivator is an attitude of ***consideration*** on the part of the boss toward the employee. Whenever an employee feels that the boss cares about him as a person rather than just as an employee, he feels more valuable and performs his job better.

The Law of Indirect Effort

The secret to building and maintaining wonderful friendships and relationships is simple. It is for you to practice the Law of Indirect Effort in every interaction with other people.

You must get out of yourself and your own preoccupations in order to get into other people and how they might be thinking and feeling.

Therefore, if you want to have a friend, you must first *be* a friend. If you want people to like you, you should first ***like them.*** If you want people to respect you, you should first ***respect them.*** If you want to impress others, you should first ***be impressed by them.*** In this way, by approaching people indirectly, you appeal to their deepest subconscious needs.

Raise Other People's Self-Esteem

The deepest subconscious need that people have is the need to feel ***important.*** Since you have this need as well, whenever you practice the Law of Indirect Effort and focus on making other people feel important, you reinforce their self-image, increase their self-esteem, and make them feel happy about themselves—and by extension, about yourself.

Whenever you say or do anything to raise the self-esteem of another person, you trigger a "boomerang" effect that causes your own self-esteem to go up at the same time and in the same measure. You can never do or say anything to make another person feel better about himself without simultaneously feeling better about yourself.

It takes tremendous self-discipline and self-control for you to rise above yourself. Instead of trying to get other people to like you and be impressed by you, focus first on liking them and being impressed by them.

Seven Ways to Make People Feel Important

The key to excellent relationships with others is quite simple: Make them feel important. To the degree to which you can make other people feel important—starting with the members of your family and then extending outward to your friends and coworkers—you will become one of the most popular people in your world.

There are seven ways to make other people feel important. These are simple practices that you can learn through repetition.

1. Accept People the Way They Are: One of the deepest cravings of human nature is to be accepted by other people without judgment, evaluation, or criticism. Psychologists call this behavior "unconditional positive regard." This is when you accept the other person completely, without reservation, for exactly the way he or she is.

Because most people are judgmental and critical, to be unconditionally accepted by another person raises that person's self-esteem, reinforces his or her self-image, and makes that person feel happy about him or herself.

In the movie, *Bridget Jones Diary*, the entire focus was on the discovery by Bridget that she had found a man "who likes me just the way I am." This was considered to be such an amazing thing to happen. All her friends were astonished that anyone could ever have a relationship based on unconditional acceptance by another person.

When you look at other people and give them a genuine smile, they feel happier about themselves. Their self-esteem goes up. They feel more valuable and important.

When you stop thinking about yourself and the impression you are making on others and instead start thinking ***about*** others and the impression they are making on you, you can relax. You take a deep breath and just smile at people when you meet them and greet them both at home and at work. It is one of the most powerful self-esteem and relationship-building behaviors you can do. Smiling at people makes them feel important and valuable.

2. Show Your Appreciation for Others: Whenever you appreciate another person for anything that he or she has done or said, you raise that person's self-esteem and make him or her feel more important. Expressions of appreciation—from small nods and smiles all the way through to cards, letters, and gifts—raise people's self-esteem and cause them to like themselves more. As a result, by the Law of Indirect Effort, they will like you more as well.

The simplest way to express appreciation is to simply say, "Thank you." The words "thank you" are deeply appreciated in any language, anywhere in the world. I have traveled in ninety countries, and the very first thing I do is learn the words for "please" and "thank you." Each time you use those words, people brighten up, smile, and feel happy to be in your presence.

Every time you say thank you, it has an almost magical effect on the other person. It makes him feel important and far happier about being in your presence and helping you with anything you need.

3. Be Agreeable: The most welcomed people in every situation are those who are generally agreeable and positive with others. On the other hand, argumentative people who question, complain, and disagree are seldom welcome anywhere.

When you nod, smile, and agree with another person when he or she is talking or expressing an opinion, you make that person feel intelligent, respected, valuable, and important. When you are agreeable with another person, even if he says something with which you may not be in complete accord, you make that person feel happy to be in your presence.

In my work as a professional speaker, I meet thousands of people each year. They come up to me and often express opinions on subjects on which I am often well informed and they obviously are not. Sometimes they say ridiculous things that are either not true or make no sense.

In every case, however, I smile and agree, nodding and asking them questions and listening to them express their ideas and opinions. They go away feeling that they have had a good conversation with the speaker and that I probably agree with them. It costs me nothing and it makes them happy. It makes them feel important.

4. Show Your Admiration: People usually invest a lot of personal emotion in their possessions, traits, and accomplishments. When you admire something belonging to another person, it makes him feel happy about himself. As Abraham Lincoln said, "Everybody likes a compliment."

Express your admiration for people's appearance and specific items of their clothing or dress. Men are especially complimented when you say something nice about their ties or their shoes. Women enjoy being complimented about their hair or any other item of their appearance. People spend a lot of time putting themselves together before they go out.

You can also compliment a person's traits or characteristics, saying things such as, "You are certainly persistent." People invest their entire lives developing traits and qualities—especially positive qualities—and they feel flattered when you notice and compliment them on those qualities.

Compliment a person's accomplishments. Tell people how much you admire their home or office or the business they have built or the position they have achieved in that business.

5. Pay Attention to Others: Perhaps the most powerful way to raise another person's self-esteem is to listen to him attentively when he speaks. In my book ***The Power of***

Charm, my coauthor Ron Arden and I explain how listening to a person while he talks on any subject in a way that is focused is perceived as charming behavior.

The key to great listening is for you to ask questions and then hang on every word of the answers. When the person slows down or comes to the end of a statement, ask another question. Lean forward attentively. Listen without interrupting. Listen as though what the person is saying is the smartest and most interesting thing you have ever heard.

When people are attentively listened to, their brain releases endorphins. As a result, they feel happy about themselves. Their self-esteem goes up. What's more, they associate this happy feeling with being in your presence. From this, a person will like you more and find you a more interesting and intelligent person.

*6. **Never Criticize, Condemn, or Complain*** about anything, whether it be directly or indirectly. Never do or say anything that lowers a person's self-esteem or makes him feel less important or valuable. Refuse to gossip or discuss other people in a negative way. Never say anything about a person that you would not say to his face.

The most harmful force in all of human relationships is ***destructive criticism.*** It lowers a person's self-esteem, makes him feel angry and defensive, and causes him to dislike the source. So never complain about people or situations that you don't like.

The most common word to describe the most popular people in every field is the word "nice." When you think of a business that you like to patronize or a restaurant you like to visit, you always think of the people there as being "nice." Whenever you recommend or refer someone to someone else, you always mention that he or she is a "nice person."

In sales and business, the nice people are always the most successful. People like to buy from them, buy again, and then recommend them to their friends. People enjoy seeing nice people, and they look forward to seeing them again.

When asked what they mean by the word "nice," people say that he or she is "cheerful." The more positive you are, the more cheerful you are likely to be. The more cheerful you are, the nicer personality you will have. The nicer personality you have, the more people will look forward to seeing you and being around you.

*7. **Be Courteous, Concerned, and Considerate of Everyone You Meet:*** Think of these as "the three Cs" and practice them with everyone you meet.

When you treat a person with ***courtesy*** and respect, he or she feels more valuable and important. As a result of making a person feel more valuable and respected, that person will in turn value and respect you even more as well.

When you express ***concern*** about things that are happening in a person's life, he warms up to you and likes you more. When a person has a difficult situation and you express your concern or compassion, you touch his heart.

You connect with his emotions. Through this, you make yourself a more likable person.

Consideration is the third of the three Cs. When you practice consideration, you discipline yourself to do and say things to people that makes them feel more valuable and important.

Be Concerned About Other People

When you meet people for the first time or again after a period of time, ask them how they are, and then listen closely to the answers. People will often share with you a concern or problem in their lives. When they do, practice consideration and sensitivity. Treat the problem or difficulty as though it were extremely important to you. Amazingly enough, when you act as if you are really interested and concerned with a problem or situation in another person's life, you very soon start to feel genuinely affected emotionally by the other person.

The rule for building lifelong friendships and wonderful relationships is simple. Resolve that from now on, when people leave your presence, they will feel much ***better*** than they did when they entered your presence. Practice all the ideas above to make people feel important. Look for ways to raise people's self-esteem and reinforce their self-image. Make them feel as though they are valuable and worthwhile. Furthermore, everything that you do or say to make another person feel important makes you feel important as well.

Action Exercises:

1. Make a list of the most important friends in your work and personal life. What could you do to make them feel better about themselves?
2. Identify the first thing you could do in every meeting or encounter to make the other person feel important.
3. Resolve to make each person feel more valuable and worthwhile because he or she spoke to you.
4. Practice nonjudgmentalism in all your relationships. Always assume the best of intentions on the part of others.
5. Imagine that each person you meet has only a short time to live and you are the only person who knows.
6. Find something about each person that is impressive to you, and then tell the other person how impressed you are.
7. Imagine that there is a hidden camera and microphone recording every interaction you have with other people. How would you behave differently?

Chapter 21

Self-Discipline and Peace of Mind

"Men are anxious to improve their circumstances, but are unwilling to improve themselves; they therefore remain bound. The man who does not shrink from self-crucifixion can never fail to accomplish the object upon which his heart is set. This is true of earthly as of heavenly things. Even the man whose object is to acquire wealth must be prepared to make great personal sacrifices before he can accomplish his object; and how much more so he who would realize a strong and well-poised life."

—JAMES ALLEN

You require high levels of self-discipline if you truly desire to develop all your inner resources and fulfill your true potential. Throughout the ages, in all religions and philosophies the highest human good or idea has been ***peace of mind.*** Your ability to achieve your own peace of mind is the true measure of your success and the key determinant of your happiness.

To develop spiritually, and to become a fully functioning person, you must regularly apply self-discipline and self-control to your thoughts, feelings, and actions. Spiritual development, inner peace, and the experience of joy all require self-mastery and self-control.

• • •

Outer Versus Inner Success

To succeed in the "outer world," you must ***discipline*** yourself to focus and concentrate, work hard at your job, take continuous action toward your goals, and become better and more capable as you move onward and upward in life.

To succeed in the "inner world," however, requires almost the ***opposite*** abilities. To achieve inner peace, you must discipline yourself to let go of everything that can disrupt your sense of inner peace and contentment.

Zen Buddhism teaches that the main cause of human suffering and unhappiness is "attachment." People become attached to ideas, opinions, and material things, and then they are reluctant to let go of them. Sometimes people become so preoccupied with these external factors that it affects their mental and physical health—even keeping them awake at night.

When you practice detachment, separating yourself ***emotionally*** from things or outcomes, the negative emotions involved stop as well, like unplugging a light from the socket.

The Need to Be Right

Most people have a deep down need to be right. However, when you stop caring if you are right or wrong, all the emotions surrounding this need for rightness disappear. Dr. Gerald Jampolsky asked the great question: "Do you want to be right, or do you want to be happy?"

Some people become passionate about their political or religious beliefs, all of which have been ***learned*** from someone else in some way. But when you put those beliefs aside for a while, they lose their ability to stir your emotions or to inflame your anger.

I have friends and meet people with ideas and opinions that range all over the political and religious spectrums. In most cases, we get along well together because we simply put aside the discussion of opinions on which we differ. We consciously and deliberately ***discipline ourselves*** to detach from these ideas, and we focus instead on subjects that we agree on and in which we share common interests.

Refuse to Blame Anyone for Anything

The chief cause of negative emotions and the primary destroyer of inner peace is ***blame***. As I mentioned earlier in the book, it is not possible to have a negative emotion without having someone or something to blame in some way or for something.

Blame requires one or both of two factors to exist. The first is ***identification***. This occurs when you take something personally: You identify with it. As soon as you decide to feel that someone has done or said something negative that affects your personal interests in some way, you immediately become angry and blame that person.

Even if someone who is hurrying to work, completely preoccupied, and who may have just had a fight with his or her spouse accidentally cuts you off in traffic, you can immediately become angry at that person, a complete stranger, because you took his driving behavior *personally*.

But when you ***discipline yourself*** to detach and stop taking things personally, the negative emotional charge connected with the person or incident stops almost immediately. For example, when someone cuts you off in traffic, you can detach from the situation emotionally by saying to yourself, "Oh well, he's probably in a hurry to get to work. Maybe he's late."

The minute you say that to yourself, all negativity associated with the event vanishes and you become calm, relaxed, and positive once more.

Give Up Your Suffering

The second root cause of blaming is ***justification***. This occurs when you tell yourself (and others) why it is that you are entitled to be angry or upset in this situation.

Many people fall in love with their ***suffering***. Their past problems become a primary focus of their lives. They think about what happened all the time. They go through the day and even the night carrying on angry conversations with people who are not present, people who they feel have hurt them in the past.

Whenever they get into a conversation for any period of time, they bring out their suffering, like a trader in a bazaar, and display it to the other person. They then recycle through the unhappy events of their lives, telling what happened, how they were badly treated, and how awful the other person was to have behaved in this way.

However, when you ***discipline yourself*** to stop justifying your negative emotions by continually rehashing what happened and what the other person did or didn't do, and when you instead calmly accept that "stuff happens" in life, your negativity accompanying the other person or situation dies away.

Practice Forgiveness

The height of self-discipline in spiritual development is the practice of forgiveness. The Law of Forgiveness says that "you are mentally and emotionally healthy to the degree that you can freely forgive anyone who has hurt you in any way."

Every person—including you—has experienced destructive criticism, negative treatment, unkindness, rudeness, unfairness, betrayal, and dishonesty from others over the years. These events are unfortunate, but they are an inevitable and unavoidable part of being a member of the human race. The only way you can avoid the problems and difficulties of living in a busy society with many different kinds of people is to live in a cave.

The only question you need to ask and answer after you have had a negative experience is "How long will it take me to get over this event and get on with my life?" This is a decision only you can make. It is one of the most important types of decisions that you make in your own life if you truly want to be happy. What's more, it is a true test of your mental and spiritual discipline.

The Forgetting Curve

Each person has a "Forgetting Curve," or what is often called a "Forgiveness Curve." This curve measures how quickly you forgive and forget a negative experience, and it determines how mentally and emotionally healthy you really are.

Imagine a rectangle with a scale from zero to one hundred ascending the left side of the rectangle. This is the scale of the intensity of the negative emotion you experience when you are hurt or offended in some way. Across the bottom of this graph are the months and years of your life.

You can have either a flat forgiveness curve or a steep, downward sloping forgiveness curve. If your forgiveness curve is flat, this means that you continue to be angry for a long time, sometimes for years or even decades at the same level as when the event occurred.

There are countless people who are still angry about something one of their parents did or said to them decades ago. Furthermore, they will tell you about it at the drop of a hat. They will reach into their gunnysack of unforgiven events and pull out their childhood experiences and share them with you.

Every psychologist and psychiatrist who deal with unhappy people are employed because their patients have flat forgiveness curves. Their primary conversation in therapy is talking about what someone did or didn't do to them or for them at some point in the past—and how unhappy that person still feels about it today.

Get Over It and Get On with It

Truly healthy people, on the other hand, have ***downward*** sloping forgiveness curves. They have had just as many difficulties and problems in life as anyone else, but they have ***disciplined themselves*** by resolving to forgive and forget quickly so they can get on with their lives. They refuse to gunnysack their problems and carry them forward. They simply let them go and turn their attention to the things that make them happy.

The discipline of forgiveness is the key to the spiritual kingdom. It is only possible for you to enjoy high levels of peace of mind when you develop the habit and discipline of freely forgiving other people for everything and anything that they have done to hurt you.

Forgiveness Is Selfish

Some people are confused about the concept of forgiveness. They think that forgiving someone else for having hurt them is the same as ***condoning*** that behavior, or even approving of it. Quite the contrary. Forgiveness is a purely ***selfish*** act. Forgiveness has nothing whatever to do with the ***other*** person. You forgive others so that ***you*** yourself can be emotionally free, so that you no longer carry that baggage around with you.

You have a wonderful mind. You are incredibly intelligent and insightful. You can use your mind on your behalf in order to help you to be joyous and happy or you can use it ***against*** yourself. The way you use your mind at the highest level is to find reasons to forgive others. Instead of rehashing and dissecting a past event, looking for rationalizations, justifications, and reasons to take something personally, use your intelligence to find reasons to accept responsibility and let go of the negative situation.

Accept Responsibility and Forgive

The instant you accept responsibility and forgive everyone for anything that they ever did to hurt you in any way, you liberate yourself completely. All your negative emotions disappear. In place of your negative emotions, you experience a sense of inner peace, love, happiness, and joy.

The payoff for using your self-discipline to practice forgiveness on an ongoing basis is extraordinary. When you use your incredible abilities of self-control, self-mastery, and detachment to separate yourself emotionally from situations that would otherwise make you unhappy, the entire quality of your life improves in a wonderful way.

Action Exercises:

1. Take the forgiveness test: Do you want to be right or do you want to be happy?

2. Identify the people from your past who you feel have hurt you in any way, and then make a decision today to forgive them and let go of those negative feelings.
3. Find reasons ***not*** to justify your negative emotions of blame or anger, and instead, use your intelligence to accept responsibility.
4. Set peace of mind as your highest goal, and then resolve to let go of any thoughts or emotions that disturb you in any way.
5. Begin today to read something spiritual and uplifting each morning before you begin your day. This habit will change your life.
6. From now on, refuse to take things personally. Ask yourself how much it will matter five years from today.
7. Practice the Buddhist method of detachment from money and material things, and refuse to become upset or worried about anything.